T0301504

Entrepreneurial Personality and Small Business Management

Entrepreneurial Personality and Small Business Management

Is there a Narcissist in Every Successful Entrepreneur?

Simona Leonelli

Research Fellow, Department of Economics and Management, University of Padova, Italy

Francesca Masciarelli

Associate Professor, Department of Business Administration, University G. d'Annunzio, Italy

Edward Elgar
PUBLISHING

Cheltenham, UK • Northampton, MA, USA

Published by
Edward Elgar Publishing Limited
The Lypiatts
15 Lansdown Road
Cheltenham
Glos GL50 2JA
UK

Edward Elgar Publishing, Inc.
William Pratt House
9 Dewey Court
Northampton
Massachusetts 01060
USA

A catalogue record for this book
is available from the British Library

This book is available electronically in the **Elgar**online
Business subject collection
http://dx.doi.org/10.4337/9781839108976

ISBN 978 1 83910 896 9 (cased)
ISBN 978 1 83910 897 6 (eBook)

Printed and bound by CPI Group (UK) Ltd, Croydon CR0 4YY

Contents

Figures

Tables

Foreword

After a few decades of seeing the field of entrepreneurship trying to shed light on the personality traits of small or medium-sized enterprise (SME) managers and entrepreneurs, Bill Gartner said in 1988 that asking "Who is an entrepreneur?" was the wrong question. He suggested that researchers should focus instead on understanding how a person manages to start a business, thereby opening up the behavioral approach to entrepreneurship.

If Bill has the merit of laying the foundations of a new research perspective in entrepreneurship, it has nevertheless been necessary to wait for more than ten years before seeing works on entrepreneurial personality become "à la mode". At the turn of the 2000s, academic journals began to publish a series of meta-analyses that demonstrated that personality was linked to the entrepreneurial career. Even further, Scott Shane and colleagues (2010, 2015) demonstrated that not only does personality affect vocational choice, but that the genetics underlying the personality structure also explain entrepreneurship as a career choice. To simplify, entrepreneurs are probably born with a strong potentiality that will influence their choices and their performance.

Although they did not revive research by suggesting new avenues related to the personality of entrepreneurs, with the exception of Shane and colleagues in genetics (2010, 2015), these works have demonstrated the importance of the personality to the entrepreneurial career, allowing the subject to be restored to its former glory in the field of entrepreneurship. It is in this context of renewed interest in entrepreneurial personality that the work of Simona Leonelli and Francesca Masciarelli takes on its full relevance.

I remember very well when, a decade ago, my colleague Cynthia Mathieu, a psychologist specializing in organizational behavior, suggested that we should study the narcissism of entrepreneurs. At first glance, I was skeptical: most of the entrepreneurship field saw entrepreneurs as mythical heroes, leading researchers to focus on the positive aspects of entrepreneurship, including the brighter sides of personality associated with this career.

However, for my colleague Cynthia, who was not used to studying entrepreneurs and publishing in entrepreneurship journals, it was crystal clear: "You only have to talk with them for less than ten minutes to realize that it is obvious that they are more narcissistic than the general population!" And she was right! At that time, apart from a few works here and there, notably the work carried out by Kets de Vries (1985) on the darker aspects of entrepreneurship, few researchers focused on these dimensions. That was a very promising idea to follow!

Since then, we have witnessed a true outpouring of works on these issues. This situation also forces us to carry out a new reading of the phenomenon of personality in entrepreneurship by also integrating the darker aspects of personality – in particular, narcissism. In this context, the magnificent work of Simona and Francesca is timely in offering us an in-depth review of the knowledge on the thematic, combined with very novel results and new perspectives that allow us to see what remains to be done in that direction.

Another important contribution of this book is to avoid being fooled by what can be classified as "dark" or "bright" traits. In the end, everything is a question of context. Being a pleasant person is generally perceived as a good quality, a positive aspect of personality in several contexts. However, when it is time to negotiate, a talented person in the negotiation would probably be less agreeable than the average person, as the negotiation process involves, mostly if not always, being unpleasant in order to succeed.

The authors go beyond simplistic analyses and take the perspective of the impact of entrepreneurial personality to another level. More specifically, they turn their attention to narcissism, the study of which has grown in recent years, especially in the field of entrepreneurship. So far, many recent works have highlighted that narcissism can trigger intention and action and that it affects many dimensions of management, especially leadership. They go further in showing how narcissism affects many different aspects of the entrepreneurial process.

Globally, this book sheds important light on the role of the personality in various processes relating to entrepreneurship and in the development of firms. The two authors illustrate how personality affects the innovation process, the entrepreneurial orientation, the search for financing, and certain aspects related to the entrepreneurial career. In this sense, it contributes significantly to opening up new horizons of research on the role of personality in entrepreneurship, in particular with regard to the "darker" facets such as narcissism. It is, therefore, a "must-read" for anyone interested in the personality of entrepreneurs. There is no doubt that this book will set the cat among the pigeons on these questions and will be of great help in imagining the future of research on entrepreneurial personality.

REFERENCES

Gartner, W. B. (1988). Who is an entrepreneur? Is the wrong question. *American Journal of Small Business, 12*(4), 11–32.

Kets de Vries, M. F. (1985). The dark side of entrepreneurship. *Harvard Business Review, 63*(6), 160–167.

Shane, S., & Nicolaou, N. (2015). Creative personality, opportunity recognition and the tendency to start businesses: A study of their genetic predispositions. *Journal of Business Venturing, 30*(3), 407–419.

Shane, S., Nicolaou, N., Cherkas, L., & Spector, T. D. (2010). Genetics, the Big Five, and the tendency to be self-employed. *Journal of Applied Psychology, 95*(6), 1154–1162.

Étienne St-Jean, PhD
Full Professor
Université du Québec à Trois-Rivières

Acknowledgments

We want to thank all the people who, in different ways, believed in us. All of them have encouraged us to move forward. All of them have stimulated us to improve and carry on our research activities and projects and, finally, to write this book.

We would like to express our thankfulness to Professor Federica Ceci (University G. d'Annunzio), who helped us to get to know each other and work together; she served as a mediator in troubled times and helped us with her comments and helpful feedback. We would like to express our gratitude to Professors Paolo Gubitta (University of Padova), Diego Campagnolo (University of Padova), Andrea Prencipe (LUISS Guido Carli), Vangelis Souitaris (Cass Business School), Augusta Consorti (University G. d'Annunzio), and Michelina Venditti (University G. d'Annunzio), who believed and supported us during our research; they are a continuous flow of inspiration and scholarly suggestions.

Our thanks to Claudia Iannessa, who corrected and edited the whole manuscript and to everyone on the Edward Elgar Publishing team who helped us so much. Special thanks to Ellen Pearce and Francine O'Sullivan who dedicated their valuable time to share their knowledge and experience with us.

We would like to thank all the entrepreneurs and fieldworkers who have given so freely of their time and expertise during our research.

We would like to thank our friends and colleagues who have accompanied us along our journey and who have enriched our life and work. Thanks goes to Dr Valentina Battista, Dr Marcella Marra, Professor Antonio D'Andreamatteo, Professor Fabrizia Fontana, Professor Martina Gianechini, Dr Alessandra Tognazzo. We are very grateful for their friendship and advice.

On a final note, our special thanks go to the people we love the most:

Simona:
I must start by thanking my awesome husband, Emanuele. He supported me every day, and in this project he gave us precious advice on the book cover. Thanks to my parents, my cousin Ilaria, and all my family; despite

the distance they always support me and are in touch with me, being part of my day-to-day life.

Francesca:
I would like to thank my beautiful daughter, Beatrice, my amazing husband Carlo, my lovely parents, Adalgisa and Oreste, and all my family for the support and encouragement they have given me.

1. Introduction to entrepreneurial narcissism

1.1 THE MYTH OF NARCISSUS

Here the boy, exhausted by the efforts of hunting and the heat, came to lie down, attracted by the beauty of the place and the source, but while trying to calm the thirst, another thirst is born to him. Kidnapped in drinking from the image he sees reflected, falls in love with a chimera: a body that is only shadow. Astonished he stares at himself and without being able to take his eyes off it remains petrified as a statue carved in Paro marble. Lying on the ground, he contemplates those two stars that are his eyes, hair worthy of Bacchus, worthy even of Apollo, and smooth cheeks, ivory neck, the beauty of the mouth, the pink suffused on the snow-white, and all he admires is what makes him wonderful. Desires, ignoring him, himself, lover and loved object, while he craves, he craves, and at the same time he lights and burns. How many times he throws useless kisses at the fiction of the source! How many times does he dip his arms in water to throw them around the neck he sees and that is not grasped in the water! (Publio Ovidio Nasone, *Metamorphoses*)

Narcissism, whose common concept is represented by self-adoration, is a subject of long-standing human fascination. The myth of Narcissus is certainly the best known in Greek mythology. It is so famous that it has become a word in common use, indicating a distinct trait of an individual: the immeasurable love for oneself. The myth of Narcissus tells the story of a beautiful young man who loses his life by falling madly in love with his own reflection. Clearly, the popular view only touches the surface of a vast and complicated phenomenon.

Narcissism has become a defining feature of the modern era: interest in the concept has captured the imagination of the public, media, and literature. In the 1970s, the American journalist Tom Wolfe coined the phrase "the 'me' decade" to describe a rise in the celebration of the self (Wolfe, 1976), and the American historian and social critic Christopher Lasch (1979) published *The Culture of Narcissism*, which explored the emergence of narcissistic entitlement and decadence. These popularized texts have been paralleled by a growing body of academic interest and empirical research, particularly in the fields of psychology, social science, and cultural studies. Within psychiatry, the concept of narcissism has evolved from early psychoanalytic theorizing to its official inclusion as a personality disorder in psychiatric nomenclature.

Havelock Ellis was the first theoretician to use the myth of Narcissus to describe narcissism as a clinical entity, in his description of states of intense autoerotism or preoccupation with one's own sexual body (Ellis, 1898). Psychoanalysts subsequently elaborated the construct of narcissism as a personality characteristic of vanity and self-love that is neither exclusively sexual nor confined to the realm of pathology, but a normal part of human development. Otto Rank (1911) wrote the first psychoanalytic paper focusing on narcissism, which was followed by the publication of Freud's now classic text *On Narcissism* (Freud, 1914 [1991]). These works highlighted the defensive function of narcissism in protecting the individual from feelings of low self-worth and self-esteem, as well as conceptualizing narcissism as a dimensional psychological state that ranges from normal to pathological, forerunning the ideas introduced by more contemporary personality trait theorists (Levy, Ellison, & Reynoso, 2011).

1.2   THE PERSONALITY OF THE ENTREPRENEUR

Entrepreneurship is a process that affects economic growth, innovation, and employment; therefore, it is an important and widely researched topic in the field of management (Decker, Calo, & Weer, 2012). Within this field, previous studies have explored the role of the entrepreneur by analyzing their personal characteristics (Korunka, Frank, Lueger, & Mugler, 2003; Leonelli, Ceci, & Masciarelli, 2016; Leonelli, Masciarelli, & Fontana, 2019; Mathieu & St-Jean, 2013), attitudes (Block, Sandner,

& Spiegel, 2013; Desimoni & Leone, 2014; Leonelli et al., 2019), behaviors, and qualities (Gardiner & Jackson, 2015; Hatak, Harms, & Fink, 2015; Matzler, Bauer, & Mooradian, 2015), and how these can lead to entrepreneurial success (Markman & Baron, 2003; Rauch & Frese, 2000, 2007).

In this book we will focus on the personality of the entrepreneur. Entrepreneurial personality helps to clarify why entrepreneurs act differently when facing similar situations, as well as the reason that some entrepreneurs are more successful than others (Leonelli et al., 2016; Nga & Shamuganathan, 2010). An individual's personality defines the person and it tends not to change over time (Vitelli, 2014).

It has been shown that personality traits such as optimism, locus of control, self-esteem, conscientiousness, and narcissism are crucial to entrepreneurial achievement (Baum & Locke, 2004; Cooper, Gimeno-Gascon, & Woo, 1994; Kee & Chye, 1993; Kickul & Zaper, 2000). However, a comprehensive understanding of how entrepreneurial personality shapes small business outcomes remains elusive. Identifying whether and how the entrepreneurial personality affects small firms would be a major contribution to management science, and entrepreneurship research in particular. Describing entrepreneurial personality traits is essential to understanding the way small firms create value (Mitchell et al., 2002; Wales, Patel, & Lumpkin, 2013; Wallace, Little, Hill, & Ridge, 2010). In the case of small firms, entrepreneurs have a greater impact on firm strategy; in larger organizations, firm size can increase the distance between decision-maker personality and firm outcome (DeTienne, 2010). In larger firms, decision-makers are more likely to delegate decision authority (Graham, Harvey, & Puri, 2015), and the presence of several hierarchical levels might mediate the effect of the decision-maker's personality on results.

In this book, we will analyze both the bright and the dark sides of entrepreneurial personality, with a focus on entrepreneurial narcissism. Among the many personality traits identified in the literature, we will explore the role of the so-called Big Five personality traits (i.e., openness to experience, conscientiousness, extraversion, agreeableness, and neuroticism), the locus of control (i.e., internal and external), and the Dark Triad (i.e., narcissism, Machiavellianism, and psychopathy). In our book, all these traits will be conceived of as personality dimensions without considering them in relation to their extreme manifestations, which can be seen as personality disorders. Following prior studies, those traits can be categorized as bright or dark (Resick, Whitman, Weingarden, &

Hiller, 2009; Smith, Hill, Wallace, Recendes, & Judge, 2017). In general, bright traits are beneficial for individuals and firms, while dark traits are considered detrimental (Judge & LePine, 2007). Bright traits include openness to experience – the tendency to be creative and perceptive; conscientiousness – being respectful of the rules and being organized; extraversion – the tendency to be outgoing, active, and enthusiastic; agreeableness – being kind, altruistic, and trusting (Zhao & Seibert, 2006); and internal locus of control – the perception that personal attributes and behavior drive individual outcomes (Galvin, Randel, Collins, & Johnson, 2018). Dark traits include narcissism – a sense of grandiosity, pride, egotism, and a lack of empathy (Chatterjee & Hambrick, 2007); Machiavellianism – an individual tendency to be manipulative and achieve goals using any means; psychopathy – dysfunctional interpersonal behaviors of people who employ charm and manipulative techniques for personal gain (Paulhus & Williams, 2002); neuroticism – the tendency to be anxious, fearful, and depressed (Zhao & Seibert, 2006); and external locus of control – the belief in external forces affecting individual outcomes (Galvin et al., 2018).

Previous research demonstrates that both the bright and the dark traits of an entrepreneur's personality affect small firms in different ways, as well as affecting the recognition of business opportunities (Navis & Ozbek, 2016), the exploitation of opportunities (Haynes, Hitt, & Campbell, 2015; Ucbasaran, Westhead, Wright, & Binks, 2003), and firm survival and growth (Ciavarella, Buchholtz, Riordan, Gatewood, & Stokes, 2004; Grijalva & Harms, 2014). Kickul and Gundry (2002) show that entrepreneurs with open personalities are more able to identify possibilities for developing new products and entering new markets. This personality trait facilitates firm growth and firm success through changes and transformations to organizational structures. Other authors show that extroversion and conscientiousness influence the ability to attract funding from angel investors (Murnieks, Sudek, & Wiltbank, 2015), venture capitalists (Black, Burton, Wood, & Zimbelman, 2010), and crowdfunding platforms (Bollaert, Leboeuf, & Schwienbacher, 2019).

However, scholars have recently begun to challenge the conventional belief that bright traits are always beneficial and dark traits are always detrimental, thus exploring the potential upsides of dark traits as well as the potential downsides of bright traits (Smith et al., 2017). There is some evidence suggesting that the effects of different personalities on organizations are complex. For example, extreme levels of conscientiousness – usually considered a bright trait – can lead to failure to adapt to the context (e.g., Carter, Guan, Maples, Williamson, & Miller, 2016; Judge & LePine, 2007), while higher levels of narcissism – usually considered a dark trait – might be positive in certain situations (e.g., Castille, Buckner, & Thoroughgood, 2018; Maccoby, 2003; Petrenko, Aime, Ridge, & Hill, 2016).

Narcissism occupies a large part of the book. A narcissist is defined as an individual who is arrogant, overconfident, and self-important, who sees themselves as superior and deserving of special treatment, who requires admiration, lacks empathy, is authoritarian, tends to exploit others, and overestimates his or her abilities (Campbell, Goodie, & Foster, 2004; Chatterjee & Hambrick, 2007; Rosenthal & Pittinsky, 2006; Wales et al., 2013). As stated above, the word narcissism has its origins in Greek mythology, and Freud (1914 [1991]) was the first to use the term "narcissist" to identify an individual manifesting self-admiration, self-promotion, and a tendency to see others as extensions of themselves (Chatterjee & Hambrick, 2007). This implies both negative and positive aspects of narcissism. The positive aspects include the ability of narcissists to become leaders, support others, as well as contribute to social growth with innovative inputs (Maccoby, 2000). The negative aspects include a distorted view of self-worth, grandiosity, self-centeredness, arrogance, and exploitation of interpersonal relationships. Narcissists see others only as a means to satisfy their need for admiration and reinforcement (Campbell, Reeder, Sedikides, & Elliot, 2000; Campbell, Rudich, & Sedikides, 2002). The present book is focused on entrepreneur narcissism for three main reasons. First, previous studies show that narcissism is a personality trait common to those occupying leadership positions (Engelen, Neumann, & Schmidt, 2016; Grijalva & Harms, 2014). Second, it has been demonstrated that the strategic choices made by narcissistic individuals differ systematically from the choices made by non-narcissists (Chatterjee & Hambrick, 2007). Third, within groups, narcissists tend to emerge as leaders and to be quickly perceived by others as effective and influential (Engelen et al., 2016; Judge, LePine, & Rich, 2006).

1.3   CASE STUDY: AN INTERVIEW WITH A NARCISSISTIC LEADER

The personality and behavior of the leader, the perception that followers have of the leader, and the context where this interaction takes place are dynamics involved in the leadership process (McCallum &

O'Connell, 2009). Among the many other personality traits, narcissism is often linked to the personality of a leader; this is because it is easy to identify narcissists at the top of organizations, and partly because narcissism seems well-suited to leadership (Campbell & Campbell, 2009). Leadership positions are a useful social platform for obtaining the narcissistic goals of self-enhancement and, on the other hand, sometimes followers are likely to see narcissistic personalities as leaders who need to be pleased (Deluga, 1997).

In the following, we recount an interview with a narcissistic leader, Luca Sassi (not his real name), a self-made entrepreneur who has successfully designed and implemented a pedagogic technique that stimulates the motor schemes coordinated by the brain to improve oral communication both in children and in adults. Luca Sassi proposes a treatment comprising three phases. The first requires an intensive therapy aimed at preventing the formation of the conditioned reflex of stuttering and the constitution of the word block. This phase is also designed to eliminate repetitions, prolongations, and interruptions. In the second phase, there is an intervention in the patient's behavioral psychology to eliminate performance anxiety, nervous tension, and to increase self-esteem and motivation. The last phase consists of a group therapy allowing a comparison among patients and an assessment of personal growth and the acquisition of motivation and confidence for social reintegration. For the purposes of the present study here is a part of our interview:

> Interviewer: Please, can you explain what lies behind the success of your new technique?
> Luca Sassi (LS): Unlike the conventional methods used by my peers, the new technique of treatment I devised consists of two integrated models: the first, that I can define technical, and the second, which is more psychological and impacts on cognitive and behavioral aspects. However, the most innovative factor is the relationship between the individual and me. Even the environment plays an important role, but the connection I establish with the individual is fundamental.
> Interviewer: How do you put this new technique into practice? Do you have any colleagues or employees?
> LS: For the success of my therapy, my figure is very, very relevant. The relationship I establish with the patient and my charisma make the individual trust me. I try to make him or her reflect in me to instill my motivation, my being. This reassures the patient and allows him or her to regain control of his or her life step by step. As for colleagues and workers, I can say that my collaborators are assistants. None of them can replace me, perhaps not because they are

not able, but just because what I do is very peculiar ... the power of my words and gestures, my expert figure, the way I look in patients' eyes.
Interviewer: In the end, what are the results? Are your patients satisfied?
LS: The results are very positive, and my success is expanding. I operate in 30 Italian cities and many people have asked me to create a franchise based on my method. However, this is not possible because, even if my patients could attend the same course elsewhere, the results would not be the same since I would not be there.

This interview enables us to understand the importance of the leader and how his personality impacts on performance. Indeed, positive results depend on the fact that there is a leader with specific characteristics to advise and manage the business. We are faced with a narcissistic leader ... a successful narcissistic leader.

REFERENCES

Baum, J. R., & Locke, E. A. (2004). The relationship of entrepreneurial traits, skill, and motivation to subsequent venture growth. *Journal of Applied Psychology, 89*(4), 587–598.

Black, E. L., Burton, F. G., Wood, D. A., & Zimbelman, A. F. (2010). Entrepreneurial success: Differing perceptions of entrepreneurs and venture capitalists. *The International Journal of Entrepreneurship and Innovation, 11*(3), 189–198.

Block, J., Sandner, P., & Spiegel, F. (2013). How do risk attitudes differ within the group of entrepreneurs? The role of motivation and procedural utility. *Journal of Small Business Management, 53*(1), 183–206.

Bollaert, H., Leboeuf, G., & Schwienbacher, A. (2019). The narcissism of crowd-funding entrepreneurs. *Small Business Economics*, 1–20. Retrieved from https://doi.org/10.1007/s11187-019-00145-w

Campbell, W. K., & Campbell, S. M. (2009). On the self-regulatory dynamics created by the peculiar benefits and costs of narcissism: A contextual reinforcement model and examination of leadership. *Self and Identity, 8*(2–3), 214–232.

Campbell, W. K., Goodie, A. S., & Foster, J. D. (2004). Narcissism, confidence, and risk attitude. *Journal of Behavioral Decision Making, 17*(4), 297–311.

Campbell, W. K., Reeder, G. D., Sedikides, C., & Elliot, A. J. (2000). Narcissism and comparative self-enhancement strategies. *Journal of Research in Personality, 34*(3), 329–347.

Campbell, W. K., Rudich, E. A., & Sedikides, C. (2002). Narcissism, self-esteem, and the positivity of self-views: Two portraits of self-love. *Personality and Social Psychology Bulletin, 28*(3), 358–368.

Carter, N. T., Guan, L., Maples, J. L., Williamson, R. L., & Miller, J. D. (2016). The downsides of extreme conscientiousness for psychological well-being: The role of obsessive compulsive tendencies. *Journal of Personality, 84*(4), 510–522.

Castille, C. M., Buckner, J. E., & Thoroughgood, C. N. (2018). Prosocial citizens without a moral compass? Examining the relationship between Machiavellianism and unethical pro-organizational behavior. *Journal of Business Ethics, 149*(4), 1–37.

Chatterjee, A., & Hambrick, D. C. (2007). It's all about me: Narcissistic chief executive officers and their effects on company strategy and performance. *Administrative Science Quarterly, 52*(3), 351–386.

Ciavarella, M. A., Buchholtz, A. K., Riordan, C. M., Gatewood, R. D., & Stokes, G. S. (2004). The Big Five and venture survival: Is there a linkage? *Journal of Business Venturing, 19*(4), 465–483.

Cooper, A. C., Gimeno-Gascon, F. J., & Woo, C. Y. (1994). Initial human and financial capital as predictors of new venture performance. *Journal of Business Venturing, 9*(5), 371–395.

Decker, W. H., Calo, T. J., & Weer, C. H. (2012). Affiliation motivation and interest in entrepreneurial careers. *Journal of Managerial Psychology, 27*(3), 302–320.

Deluga, R. J. (1997). Relationship among American presidential charismatic leadership, narcissism, and rated performance. *The Leadership Quarterly, 8*(1), 49–65.

Desimoni, M., & Leone, L. (2014). Openness to experience, honesty–humility and ideological attitudes: A fine-grained analysis. *Personality and Individual Differences, 59*, 116–119.

DeTienne, D. R. (2010). Entrepreneurial exit as a critical component of the entrepreneurial process: Theoretical development. *Journal of Business Venturing, 25*(2), 203–215.

Ellis, H. (1898). Auto-eroticism: A psychological study. *Alienist and Neurologist, 19*, 260–299.

Engelen, A., Neumann, C., & Schmidt, S. (2016). Should entrepreneurially oriented firms have narcissistic CEOs? *Journal of Management, 42*(3), 698–721.

Freud, S. (1914 [1991]). On narcissism: An introduction. In J. Sandler, E. Spector Person, & P. Fonagy (Eds.), *Freud's "On narcissism: An introduction"* (standard ed., pp. 3–32). New Haven, CT: Yale University Press.

Galvin, B. M., Randel, A. E., Collins, B. J., & Johnson, R. E. (2018). Changing the focus of locus (of control): A targeted review of the locus of control literature and agenda for future research. *Journal of Organizational Behavior, 39*(7), 820–833.

Gardiner, E., & Jackson, C. J. (2015). Personality and learning processes underlying maverickism. *Journal of Managerial Psychology, 30*(6), 726–740.

Graham, J. R., Harvey, C. R., & Puri, M. (2015). Capital allocation and delegation of decision-making authority within firms. *Journal of Financial Economics, 115*(3), 449–470.

Grijalva, E., & Harms, P. D. (2014). Narcissism: An integrative synthesis and dominance complementarity model. *The Academy of Management Perspectives, 28*(2), 108–127.

Hatak, I., Harms, R., & Fink, M. (2015). Age, job identification, and entrepreneurial intention. *Journal of Managerial Psychology, 30*(1), 38–53.

Haynes, K. T., Hitt, M. A., & Campbell, J. T. (2015). The dark side of leadership: Towards a mid-range theory of hubris and greed in entrepreneurial contexts. *Journal of Management Studies, 52*(4), 479–505.

Judge, T. A., & LePine, J. A. (2007). The bright and dark sides of personality: Implications for personnel selection in individual and team contexts. In J. Legan-Fox & R. J. Klimoski (Eds.), *Research companion to the dysfunctional workplace: Management challenges and symptoms* (pp. 332–355). Cheltenham, UK and Northampton, MA, USA: Edward Elgar Publishing.

Judge, T. A., LePine, J. A., & Rich, B. L. (2006). Loving yourself abundantly: Relationship of the narcissistic personality to self- and other perceptions of workplace deviance, leadership, and task and contextual performance. *Journal of Applied Psychology, 91*(4), 762–776.

Kee, C. K., & Chye, K. H. (1993). Personality characteristics of entrepreneurs: A test on the locals at the Singapore International Monetary Exchange. *Journal of Small Business & Entrepreneurship, 10*(3), 59–68.

Kickul, J., & Gundry, L. (2002). Prospecting for strategic advantage: The proactive entrepreneurial personality and small firm innovation. *Journal of Small Business Management, 40*(2), 85–97.

Kickul, J., & Zaper, J. A. (2000). Untying the knot: Do personal and organizational determinants influence entrepreneurial intentions? *Journal of Small Business & Entrepreneurship, 15*(3), 57–77.

Korunka, C., Frank, H., Lueger, M., & Mugler, J. (2003). The entrepreneurial personality in the context of resources, environment, and the startup process: Configurational approach. *Entrepreneurship Theory and Practice, 28*(1), 23–42.

Lasch, C. (1979). *The culture of narcissism: American life in an age of diminishing expectations.* New York, NY: Warner Books.

Leonelli, S., Ceci, F., & Masciarelli, F. (2016). The importance of entrepreneurs' traits in explaining start-ups' innovativeness. *Sinergie: Italian Journal of Management, 34*(101), 71–85.

Leonelli, S., Masciarelli, F., & Fontana, F. (2019). The impact of personality traits and abilities on entrepreneurial orientation in SMEs. *Journal of Small Business & Entrepreneurship.* Retrieved from https://doi.org/10.1080/08276331.2019.1666339

Levy, K. N., Ellison, W. D., & Reynoso, J. S. (2011). A historical review of narcissism and narcissistic personality. In W. K. Campbell & J. D. Miller (Eds.), *The handbook of narcissism and narcissistic personality disorder: Theoretical approaches, empirical findings, and treatments* (pp. 3–13). Hoboken, NJ: John Wiley & Sons, Inc.

Maccoby, M. (2000). Narcissistic leaders: The incredible pros, the inevitable cons. *Harvard Business Review, 78*(1), 68–78.

Maccoby, M. (2003). *The productive narcissist: The promise and peril of visionary leadership.* New York, NY: Broadway Books.

Markman, G. D., & Baron, R. A. (2003). Person–entrepreneurship fit: Why some people are more successful as entrepreneurs than others. *Human Resource Management Review, 13*(2), 281–301.

Mathieu, C., & St-Jean, É. (2013). Entrepreneurial personality: The role of narcissism. *Personality and Individual Differences*, *55*(5), 527–531.

Matzler, K., Bauer, F. A., & Mooradian, T. A. (2015). Self-esteem and transformational leadership. *Journal of Managerial Psychology*, *30*(7), 815–831.

McCallum, S., & O'Connell, D. (2009). Social capital and leadership development: Building stronger leadership through enhanced relational skills. *Leadership & Organization Development Journal*, *30*(2), 152–166.

Mitchell, R. K., Busenitz, L., Lant, T., McDougall, P. P., Morse, E. A., & Smith, J. B. (2002). Toward a theory of entrepreneurial cognition: Rethinking the people side of entrepreneurship research. *Entrepreneurship Theory and Practice*, *27*(2), 93–104.

Murnieks, C. Y., Sudek, R., & Wiltbank, R. (2015). The role of personality in angel investing. *The International Journal of Entrepreneurship and Innovation*, *16*(1), 19–31.

Navis, C., & Ozbek, O. V. (2016). The right people in the wrong places: The paradox of entrepreneurial entry and successful opportunity realization. *Academy of Management Review*, *41*(1), 109–129.

Nga, J. K. H., & Shamuganathan, G. (2010). The influence of personality traits and demographic factors on social entrepreneurship start up intentions. *Journal of Business Ethics*, *95*(2), 259–282.

Paulhus, D. L., & Williams, K. M. (2002). The Dark Triad of personality: Narcissism, Machiavellianism, and psychopathy. *Journal of Research in Personality*, *36*(6), 556–563.

Petrenko, O. V., Aime, F., Ridge, J., & Hill, A. (2016). Corporate social responsibility or CEO narcissism? CSR motivations and organizational performance. *Strategic Management Journal*, *37*(2), 262–279.

Rank, O. (1911). Ein Beitrag zum Narzissismus [A contribution to narcissism]. In E. Bleuler & S. Freud (Eds.), *Jahrbuch für Psychoanalytische und Psychopathologische Forschungen* (Vol. 3, pp. 410–423). Leipzig/Vienna: Franz Deuticke.

Rauch, A., & Frese, M. (2000). Psychological approaches to entrepreneurial success: A general model and an overview of findings. *International Review of Industrial and Organizational Psychology*, *15*, 101–142.

Rauch, A., & Frese, M. (2007). Let's put the person back into entrepreneurship research: A meta-analysis on the relationship between business owners' personality traits, business creation, and success. *European Journal of Work and Organizational Psychology*, *16*(4), 353–385.

Resick, C. J., Whitman, D. S., Weingarden, S. M., & Hiller, N. J. (2009). The bright-side and the dark-side of CEO personality: Examining core self-evaluations, narcissism, transformational leadership, and strategic influence. *Journal of Applied Psychology*, *94*(6), 1365–1381.

Rosenthal, S. A., & Pittinsky, T. L. (2006). Narcissistic leadership. *The Leadership Quarterly*, *17*(6), 617–633.

Smith, M. B., Hill, A. D., Wallace, J. C., Recendes, T., & Judge, T. A. (2017). Upsides to dark and downsides to bright personality: A multidomain review and future research agenda. *Journal of Management*, *44*(1), 191–217.

Ucbasaran, D., Westhead, P., Wright, M., & Binks, M. (2003). Does entrepreneurial experience influence opportunity identification? *The Journal of Private Equity, 7*(1), 7–14.

Vitelli, R. (2014). *The everything guide to overcoming PTSD: Simple, effective techniques for healing and recovery.* Avon, MA: Adams Media Corporation.

Wales, W. J., Patel, P. C., & Lumpkin, G. T. (2013). In pursuit of greatness: CEO narcissism, entrepreneurial orientation, and firm performance variance. *Journal of Management Studies, 50*(6), 1041–1069.

Wallace, J. C., Little, L. M., Hill, A. D., & Ridge, J. W. (2010). CEO regulatory foci, environmental dynamism, and small firm performance. *Journal of Small Business Management, 48*(4), 580–604.

Wolfe, M. T. (1976 [2008, April 8]). The "me" decade and the third great awakening. *New York Magazine.* Retrieved from https://nymag.com/news/features/45938/

Zhao, H., & Seibert, S. E. (2006). The Big Five personality dimensions and entrepreneurial status: A meta-analytical review. *Journal of Applied Psychology, 91*(2), 259–271.

2. Understanding entrepreneurial personality

2.1 WHO IS AN ENTREPRENEUR?

The etymology of the term entrepreneur derives from the Latin word *"prehendere"*, which means "to take charge". The question "Who is an entrepreneur?" is common, and arises because there is no shared definition of who an entrepreneur is. Numerous researchers have defined an entrepreneur as someone who recognizes and explores opportunities, combining resources to gain a competitive advantage (Carland, Hoy, Boulton, & Carland, 2007; Carland, Hoy, & Carland, 1988; Hansen, Shrader, & Monllor, 2011; Huefner & Hunt, 1994). Other scholars have focused more on the complete picture of entrepreneurial action by analyzing the entrepreneurial process, including the activities and actions associated with the exploration and exploitation of opportunities (Dean & McMullen, 2007; Gartner, 1988; Klein, 2008; McMullen & Shepherd, 2006). Finally, others define entrepreneurs by emphasizing their innovative behavior, such as the introduction of new products, procedures, or the creation of new markets, characterizing their way of being (Gartner, 1990; Kang, Solomon, & Choi, 2015; Lukeš, 2013; Venkataraman, 1997).

Such a multitude of definitions indicates that there is still no standard, universally accepted definition of an entrepreneur (Gartner, 1990, 2001; McKenzie, Ugbah, & Smothers, 2007). For the purposes of this book, however, entrepreneurs are defined as individuals who create a new business to achieve profits, face risks and uncertainties, and use the necessary resources to identify opportunities and reach pre-fixed goals (Alam, 2011).

The features of the entrepreneur, venture, and environment combine to contribute to business performance (Gartner, 1985). Bird (1988) underlines the relevance of the link between the entrepreneur and the environment by supporting the importance of both the entrepreneur's temperament and disposition and the venture's external environment in targeting the entrepreneurial activity. Park (2005), on the other hand, shows that an entrepreneur decides to launch his or her business because he or she perceives the problems affecting society and wants to solve them.

In this book, we study entrepreneurs of small ventures where the so-called "founder–CEO duality" typically occurs (He, 2008; Wasserman, 2003). The founder–CEO duality manifests when the entrepreneur is both the founder and chief executive officer (CEO) of the firm (DeTienne, 2010; Gatewood, Shaver, & Gartner, 1995); therefore, he or she has the formal and informal powers for selecting the necessary resources as well as exploring and implementing new ideas (Abebe & Alvarado, 2013).

2.2   ENTREPRENEUR PERSONALITY: A LITERATURE REVIEW

Every person is characterized by both observable and unobservable traits (Brody, 2013). Observability depends on the ability to make self–other comparative judgments (e.g., "How happy are you compared to John?"), but some characteristics are difficult to represent and count (Niewiarowski & Karylowski, 2015). For these reasons, we consider observable characteristics as those that can be easily verified such as age, gender, level of education, socioeconomic background, and financial position (Hambrick & Mason, 1984). On the other hand, unobservable characteristics are personality traits that shape the individual's behavior (Plummer, 2000). In fact, personality traits are individual characteristics describing why individuals behave differently in similar situations (Leonelli, Ceci, & Masciarelli, 2016; Nga & Shamuganathan, 2010). Moreover, they include different characteristics that distinguish the individual's way of thinking, feeling, and behaving. Personality traits are stable over time; however, some traumatic events, such as divorce, death of a loved one, or job loss, can result in some changes (Cobb-Clark & Schurer, 2012).

Studies focused on entrepreneurs' observable characteristics and their effects on strategy and firms' performance do not explain why some entrepreneurs are more successful than others (Boone, Brabander, & Witteloostuijn, 1996). For this reason, a new branch of research is beginning to consider the importance of entrepreneurs' personality traits in the management and survival of small firms (O'Reilly, Caldwell, Chatman, & Doerr, 2014).

Many authors state that entrepreneurs' personality traits have a strong influence on business decisions primarily in small firms (Kickul & Gundry, 2002; Lee & Tsang, 2001; Littunen, 2000). In particular, to establish and manage new business ventures, entrepreneurs should be innovative and risk-takers; they should recognize and exploit opportunities while being able to take rapid decisions under uncertainty and resource-constrained conditions (Ardichvili, Cardozo, & Ray, 2003; Baum & Locke, 2004; Kickul & Walters, 2002; Rauch & Frese, 2007, 2014). Other studies in the entrepreneurship field have recently addressed the relationship between entrepreneur traits and firm performance. Some take entrepreneurial orientation and risk-taking behavior into account (Choe, Loo, & Lau, 2013; Hafeez, Shariff, & Lazim, 2012; Leonelli, Masciarelli, & Fontana, 2019; Zhao, Seibert, & Lumpkin, 2010), others investigate entrepreneur narcissism (Chatterjee & Hambrick, 2007; Leonelli et al., 2016; Wales, Patel, & Lumpkin, 2013), while the majority examine the Big Five personality traits (i.e., openness to experience, conscientiousness, extraversion, agreeableness, and neuroticism), all of which are characteristics representing the basic structure behind all personality traits (Ciavarella, Buchholtz, Riordan, Gatewood, & Stokes, 2004; Zhao & Seibert, 2006).

Along with all these factors that, as shown before, comprise an entrepreneur's personality, other crucial traits need to be considered. As stated above, entrepreneurs should have the necessary skills to confront situations and succeed in contexts dominated by unpredictability and anxiety elicited by new markets and projects, changes in demand, or paucity of financial resources (Nga & Shamuganathan, 2010; Smith, Hill, Wallace, Recendes, & Judge, 2017). Therefore, they should exhibit a profound passion for work. Locke (2000) observed this particular feature in business creator Bill Gates, who, thanks to his great enthusiasm, succeeded in overcoming any financial obstacle he encountered. It is possible to measure this passion with respect to the time spent by the entrepreneur in working in the firm, or with respect to his or her attachment to it. Perseverance, therefore, is an indispensable attribute for entrepreneurs. Since they often face challenging situations, they should show strength, determination, and resourcefulness. Finally, another important factor to consider is creativity, as it allows entrepreneurs to reformulate problems, express themselves easily, be flexible, and be guided by feelings and sensations (Ahlin, Drnovšek, & Hisrich, 2014). These features are not formalized as factors that can predict firm performance, but they are fundamental qualities for entrepreneurs to be able to achieve fixed goals.

Two "shades" distinguish personality traits: bright traits, that is, those seen as socially desirable, and the dark traits, that is, those seen as socially undesirable (Judge, Piccolo, & Kosalka, 2009). This bright–dark dichotomy when referring to traits is related to theory that distinguishes between bright traits that are beneficial for individuals and organizations and dark traits that are detrimental (Smith et al., 2017). However, recent studies suggest that the effects of personality in organizations are more complex. For instance, extreme levels of bright traits, such as being too conscientious, may lead to harmful outcomes (Judge & LePine, 2007), and higher levels of certain dark traits, such as narcissism, may be beneficial in certain situations (Maccoby, 2000).

In the following section, we will analyze the main personality traits before focusing on narcissism.

2.3   THE BIG FIVE MODEL

The Big Five model is a multidimensional approach to personality defini-tion through the measurement of openness to experience, conscientious-ness, extraversion, agreeableness, and neuroticism (John & Srivastava, 1999; Judge & Bono, 2000; McCrae & John, 1992). Originally dubbed by Goldberg (1983) as the Big Five, the model is the final result of a complex classification procedure aimed to develop a taxonomy for the thousands of particular attributes characterizing the human being. Costa and McCrae (1976) were the first to create a three-factor view of per-sonality – they developed the NEO Personality Inventory that accounted only for neuroticism, extraversion, and openness to experience. Later, in 1985, they added the two remaining categories, thus revising the NEO Personality Inventory and establishing the final version of the Big Five model (Costa & McCrae, 1985).

Costa and McCrae created a Big Five model that has shown robustness across cultures (Church & Lonner, 1998; McCrae & Costa, 1997), age groups (Donnellan & Lucas, 2008; Soto, John, Gosling, & Potter, 2011), and gender (Schmitt, Realo, Voracek, & Allik, 2008). It has been used in different research fields such as psychology (Buss, 1991), clinical psychology (Widiger & Costa, 1994), human resource management (Salgado, 2002), and entrepreneurship (Zhao & Seibert, 2006). To date, the Big Five is the most complete model used to identify the personality of an individual.

2.3.1   Openness to Experience

Openness describes individuals who are open-minded, intellectually curious, and who tend to seek new experiences and explore novel ideas (Costa & McCrae, 1985). This personality trait is associated with creativity, innovation, imagination, reflectivity, and untraditional thoughts. Furthermore, this personality trait is positively related to intelligence, especially in creative processes and in regard to adaptability (McCrae & Costa, 1999).

Entrepreneurs should possess this trait since it is connected with innovativeness, which is the basis of the growth and survival of small ventures. A high level of creativity is required to create new-technology ventures to satisfy particular needs that are sometimes not yet perceived. Furthermore, creativity is a valuable means to solve problems with others (Nga & Shamuganathan, 2010). Finally, openness to experience allows entrepreneurs to find new opportunities and ways to structure and develop firms (Brandstätter, 2011). This explains why openness to experience is one of the most important traits a good entrepreneur should possess (Zhao et al., 2010).

2.3.2   Conscientiousness

Conscientiousness describes individuals' degree of assiduousness, persistence, organizational skills, and goal accomplishment (Costa & McCrae, 1985). It was the first trait to be studied as it was seen as the most influential on job performance of managers and employees regardless of the task they performed. Mount and Barrick (1995) state that this personality trait comprises achievement motivation and dependability, both of which are greatly correlated with entrepreneurial activity. In particular, achievement motivation, and thus conscientiousness, stimulate entrepreneurs to be persistent and strive hard to pursue their goals, resulting in improvement in both performance and innovativeness (Brandstätter, 2011; Zhao & Seibert, 2006).

2.3.3   Extraversion

Extraversion is related to the tendency to be outgoing, assertive, active, enthusiastic, and excitement-seeking (Costa & McCrae, 1985). Extraverted people are charismatic, cheerful, and prone to entrepreneurial activity because they are in constant search of stimuli (Hafeez et al.,

2012). They love talking with people and this is fundamental in establishing social relations (Brandstätter, 2011). Extraverted individuals inspire positive feelings because they like working in groups, thus improving social interactions with colleagues and stakeholders (Zhao & Seibert, 2006). Entrepreneurs generally score highly on extroversion since they are used to dealing with people such as suppliers, venture capitalists, employees, and partners, thus developing an ability to convince people that their idea is a potentially successful one and to persuade customers to buy their products (Zhao et al., 2010). In summary, extraverted individuals enjoy talking with people and this improves their negotiation skills.

2.3.4 Agreeableness

Agreeableness defines a person who trusts, forgives, and is altruistic (Costa & McCrae, 1985). Entrepreneurs with high levels of agreeableness are cooperative and willing to strengthen interpersonal relationships. These aspects, however, can contribute both positively and negatively to entrepreneurs' capabilities. For example, entrepreneurs can develop high levels of affiliation – their peers and employees may indeed become their friends as well as colleagues. Should they need to fire someone, however, means making difficult, objective decisions regarding the team, underlining their difficulty in driving bargaining powers for their own interest (Zhao et al., 2010). Small venture entrepreneurs cannot afford low bargaining power because they need to make difficult decisions with strict time limits and in dynamic environments, and so determine firms' survival.

2.3.5 Neuroticism

Neuroticism, also known as low emotional stability, refers to individuals who tend to experience several negative emotions such as anxiety, hostility, depression, impulsiveness, and vulnerability (Costa and McCrae, 1992). Emotional volatility and worrying are viewed as obstacles for entrepreneurs (Vesper, 1990). Having a high degree of self-confidence, maintaining optimism about the results of their efforts, and strongly believing in their ability to control environmental outcomes, positively impact on firm survival (Zhao et al., 2010) and growth (Ciavarella et al., 2004). Thus, high levels of neuroticism are detrimental to entrepreneurial activity (Brandstätter, 2011; Nga & Shamuganathan, 2010).

Table 2.1   Adjectives and related behaviors of the Big Five model

Personality Traits	Adjective	Related Behaviors
Openness to experience	Curious Imaginative Plenty of interests Unconventional	*Innovative.* Individuals are cultured and always looking for new stimuli They enjoy art, music, and literature
Conscientiousness	Organized Active Calm	*Industrious.* They seek to always do their best *Efficient.* They plan in advance and are always on time
Extraversion	Energetic Adventurous Enthusiastic Outgoing	*Ambitious.* They are impetuous and, through persuasiveness, generally take on leadership roles *Sociable.* They are talkative and enjoy meeting people
Agreeableness	Confident Altruistic Disciplined Modest	*Cooperative.* They help and trust others *Considerate.* They are good-natured and cheerful. They forgive others easily
Neuroticism	Anxious Irritable Depressed Impulsive	*Insecurity.* They feel insecure about themselves and are always troubled by criticism

Source: Our elaboration based on Leonelli et al. (2016).

Table 2.1 summarizes the trait adjectives and related behaviors of the Big Five model.

2.4   LOCUS OF CONTROL

Locus of control (LOC) measures the extent to which individuals believe that events are generated by their own actions (internal locus of control) or depend on external factors they cannot control (external locus of control) (Rotter, 1954, 1966). In general, individuals with an internal LOC are usually more confident, they believe their fate is not set, and that they can influence it with their actions; on the other hand, individuals with an external LOC are more passive, as they surrender to the belief that the events in their lives are influenced by unpredictable and uncontrollable forces such as luck, fate, influential people, or institutions (Leonelli et al., 2016).

Luthans, Avey, Avolio, Norman, and Combs (2006) indicate that people with an internal LOC tend to positively face challenges and obstacles, resolving problems by seeking constructive solutions. Compared with people with an external LOC, people with an internal LOC exhibit higher achievement motivation; consequently, they are more willing to learn and enhance their capabilities and knowledge when encountering challenges (Hsiao, Lee, & Chen, 2016). Moreover, according to Asante and Affum-Osei (2019), aspiring entrepreneurs with an internal LOC are more likely to recognize entrepreneurial opportunities.

Researchers have analyzed how LOC impacts on business performance and new venture creation (see Galvin, Randel, Collins, & Johnson, 2018). Many studies show that ventures led by entrepreneurs with an internal LOC perform better than firms guided by entrepreneurs with an external LOC (Boone et al., 1996; Howell & Avolio, 1993). Other studies show that small businesses created by entrepreneurs with an internal LOC are more successful and are more likely to survive than small businesses created by entrepreneurs with an external LOC (Gatewood et al., 1995; Van de Ven, Hudson, & Schroeder, 1984).

Boone et al. (1996) also investigate the relationship between entrepreneurs' LOC and small firms' performance, showing that entrepreneurs with an internal LOC are more likely to challenge themselves in risky ventures, thus helping their firms to perform better. Also, the implementation of innovative strategies is related to entrepreneurs' internal LOC because it is a risky activity; entrepreneurs need to be confident in their skills without believing in fate as the main driving force, since this attitude discourages the implementation of innovative strategies (Miller, Kets de Vries, & Toulouse, 1982; Miller & Toulouse, 1986).

Finally, LOC strongly influences the relationship between entrepreneurs and peers and employees. Entrepreneurs with an internal LOC exploit their self-confidence to persuade and influence peers and employees, while entrepreneurs with an external LOC prefer to just give orders, imposing their point of view (Goodstadt & Hjelle, 1973; Kimmons & Greenhaus, 1976; Mitchell, Smyser, & Weed, 1975). The different ways in which entrepreneurs deal with relationships impact on firm efficiency, based on their internal or external LOC. Entrepreneurs with an internal LOC involve peers and employees in the decision-making process, making them feel they are an integral part of the firm (Gunawan & Munari, 2019). Communication and knowledge sharing in firms contribute to competitive advantage (Wang & Wang, 2012). On the other hand, entrepreneurs with an external LOC create a barrier between themselves and the other members of the firm (Agarwal & Srivastava, 2016); peers and employees must only follow directions, resulting in a lower degree of transversal thinking and responsibility-taking.

2.5   THE DARK TRIAD

Included within the category of dark traits are hubris, overconfidence, and the so-called Dark Triad, that is, narcissism, Machiavellianism, and psychopathy (Paulhus & Williams, 2002). In this book, we will focus only on the latter. The Dark Triad construct is based on the moderate positive correlations among these traits, contributing to explain both the single and the global effect (Bertl, Pietschnig, Tran, Stieger, & Voracek, 2017). To explicate, this means that each trait is positively related to the Dark Triad measure. For instance, if the level of narcissism grows, the Dark Triad measure grows. And the same follows for Machiavellianism and psychopathy. Moreover, the dark triad construct gives both a total view of the construct itself and the single impact that each personality trait has separately. Thus, these traits share both common elements and specific independent components (Paulhus, 2014; Paulhus & Williams, 2002).

Prior studies have revealed different relational patterns between the three traits and a number of variables of interest (e.g., Furnham, Richards, & Paulhus, 2013; Judge et al., 2009; Petrides, Vernon, Schermer, & Veselka, 2011). In the entrepreneurship literature, numerous authors show a positive relationship between the Dark Triad traits and entrepreneurial intention, as entrepreneurs scoring highly in the Dark Triad see the creation of the venture as a way to satisfy their need for attention and admiration (Hmieleski & Lerner, 2016; Smith et al., 2017). Other studies have demonstrated that entrepreneurs with high scores in the Dark Triad tend to be achievement oriented, and far more skilled in accumulating power, and searching for and obtaining resources (Jonason, Li, & Teicher, 2010; Jones & Figueredo, 2013). However, in the last years, there has been a call for new research streams to begin to consider the positive impact of the Dark Triad; for instance, Klotz and Neubaum (2016) ask whether the influence of these dark traits is always negative in an entrepreneurial context or can it also play a positive role in the personality–outcome relationship?

In the remainder of this section, we will analyze only two traits of the Dark Triad, namely Machiavellianism and psychopathy. Narcissism will be examined extensively in the following section.

2.5.1 Machiavellianism

The concept of Machiavellianism is derived from Niccolò Machiavelli. In his book, *Il Principe* [The Prince] (1513) Machiavelli presented people as being untrustworthy, self-serving, and malevolent, and advocated for a ruler to maintain power in an exploitative and deceitful manner. Machiavellianism was first considered as a personality trait by Christie and Geis (1970). They reviewed Machiavelli's work, classifying Machiavellianism in three dimensions: interpersonal manipulative tactics, a cynical view of human nature, and amorality. In psychological theory, Machiavellianism is defined as a complex set of personality traits, including a tendency to distrust others, a willingness to engage in amoral manipulation, a desire to maintain interpersonal control over others, and an attitude towards a status-oriented way of acting, thus representing a cynical conception of humanity (Dahling, Whitaker, & Levy, 2009; Hutter, Füller, Hautz, Bilgram, & Matzler, 2015).

Machs, namely individuals who score highly in Machiavellianism, tend to act opportunistically, amorally, and manipulatively in order to maximize their gain, often against other parties' interests (Sakalaki, Richardson, & Thépaut, 2007; Wilson, Near, & Miller, 1996; Winter, Stylianou, & Giacalone, 2004). They have a strong desire to win, even at the expense of others; they therefore generally exhibit socially deviant behaviors (e.g., lying, stealing, and cheating) (Buckels, Jones, & Paulhus, 2013; Côté, DeCelles, McCarthy, Van Kleef, & Hideg, 2011).

Machs can be described as opportunistic individuals on an economic level and, following their conviction that the ends justify the means, they have a serious urge for money, power, and competition (Hmieleski & Lerner, 2016; Sakalaki et al., 2007; Zettler & Solga, 2013). Therefore, due to their lack of moral stability and absence of emotional involvement, Machs easily disregard moral standards to pursue their own advantage, employing tactics of influence such as ingratiation and intimidation (Furnham et al., 2013). As emphasized by McHoskey, Worzel, and Szyarto (1998), external goals such as wealth, power, and status rather than intrinsic goals such as self-actualization or community and personal development strongly motivate Machs (Dahling et al., 2009). Finally, to reduce other people's power, they show an intense desire for control and an urge to dominate interpersonal situations (Hutter et al., 2015; Judge et al., 2009).

Earlier studies state that Machiavellianism is beneficial when starting an entrepreneurial career because of task orientation and an ability to perform in difficult and ambiguous situations (Fehr, Samsom, & Paulhus, 1992; Kramer, Cesinger, Schwarzinger, & Gelléri, 2011). And, recent studies show that Machiavellianism is positively related to entrepreneurial intention and entrepreneurial self-esteem (Wu, Wang, Lee, Lin, & Guo, 2019; Wu, Wang, Zheng, & Wu, 2019).

2.5.2   Psychopathy

Psychopathy is typically referred to as a personality disorder characterized by persistent antisocial behavior, impaired empathy and remorse, and disinhibited and egotistical traits (Patrick, Fowles, & Krueger, 2009), personified by serial killers, stalkers, and sadists (Marino & Tucker, 2016). Psychopaths act dysfunctionally on an interpersonal level, and they tend to charm and manipulate others in various ways for their personal purposes (Hare, 1999). The literature shows that psychopathy leads to troubled and conflicting feelings about emotions (Wu, Wang, Lee et al., 2019; Wu, Wang, Zheng et al., 2019), which results in the rejection of social norms and the constant need to oppose the status quo (Mathieu & St-Jean, 2013). Psychopathic individuals rarely experience emotional empathy, thus being capable of using other people to achieve their goals (Jonason & Krause, 2013). Furthermore, they are highly risk prone due to their dangerous insensibility to loss or risk, lacking the sometimes necessary risk avoidance associated with fear of failure (Morgan & Sisak, 2016). Ultimately, psychopaths are driven by power, prestige, and control (Deutschman, 2005), and for this reason they tend to focus on short-term benefits and on maximizing their wealth and power through short-term and hasty decisions (Boddy, 2006). Some recent studies have started to conceive of psychopathic individuals as clever, fascinating, ingenious, and even entertaining (Boddy, 2015; Mullins-Sweatt, Glover, Derefinko, Miller, & Widiger, 2010).

According to Akhtar, Ahmetoglu, and Chamorro-Premuzic (2013), some characteristics of psychopathic entrepreneurs, such as the ability to manipulate, superficiality, and lack of empathy or guilt, are positively related to entrepreneurial activity as they are attracted by exciting activities. Moreover, Crysel, Crosier, and Webster (2013) show that psychopathy and entrepreneurial success are positively related as psychopathic entrepreneurs perform well in uncertain situations.

2.6 FOCUS ON ENTREPRENEURIAL NARCISSISM

The term "narcissism" derives from the story of Narcissus, taken from Greek mythology:

> Narcissus' rejection of the love of the nymph Echo drew upon him the vengeance of the gods. They induced him to fall in love with his own reflection in the waters of a spring and he died drowning in the same river where he looked at himself. At the place where he died, a flower that bears his name sprang up.

Narcissism is generally considered a personality disorder or a pathology, but psychologists such as Emmons (1987) suggest that narcissism can be seen as a personality dimension ranging between low and high levels, and only in the presence of extreme manifestations can it be defined as a personality disorder (see also Humphreys, Haden, Novicevic, Clayton, & Gibson, 2011; Lubit, 2002).

Havelock Ellis (1898) used the term narcissism for the first time to indicate a deep and negative love of an individual for themselves. However, modern analyses of narcissism have been influenced by the considerations introduced by Freud (1914 [1991]). He defined narcissism as the way in which an individual loves themselves, considers themselves the center of the world, and often behaves spontaneously. Narcissism includes self-love, self-admiration, and the propensity to consider others as an extension of the self. By being in continuous search of affirmation, they do not consider others and their sentiments.

After Freud's definition, many scholars started to define narcissism as a personality trait. Waelder (1925) stated that narcissistic people "are condescending, they feel superior to others, they are absorbed by admiration of themselves, and they lack empathy". Other authors affirmed that narcissistic people are arrogant and presumptuous and consider themselves as more important and more capable than others. As a consequence, they think they deserve different and particular consideration and admiration, and they do not take other people's ideas and emotions into account. The narcissist has no compassion, he or she exploits others, and tends to be imperious (Chatterjee & Hambrick, 2007; Rosenthal & Pittinsky, 2006). Moreover, narcissistic individuals have a positive and inflated self-view, such as self-admiration or perverse self-love, and a self-regulatory strategy to maintain and enhance this positive self-view (Ackerman et al., 2011). Accordingly, they fantasize about fame and power, think they are special and unique, and see themselves as more intelligent and attractive than others (Campbell, Goodie, & Foster, 2004; Humphreys et al., 2011; Mathieu & St-Jean, 2013; Raskin, Novacek, & Hogan, 1991; Rosenthal & Pittinsky, 2006).

Looking through this list of definitions, narcissism appears to be an exclusively negative trait. However, it can be seen as a controversial characteristic of the individual personality since it encompasses a double connotation – a positive, that is, constructive connotation and a negative, that is, destructive connotation (de Vries, 1994; Lubit, 2002; Maccoby, 2003), which we will further investigate in the following subsections.

2.6.1   The Negative Side of Entrepreneurial Narcissism

The destructive side of narcissism corresponds to "feelings of inferiority, irrationality, an insatiable need for recognition and superiority, lack of empathy, arrogance, hypersensitivity, anger, amorality, and paranoia" (Rosenthal & Pittinsky, 2006). In detail, narcissism ranges between two sets of features – vulnerability and grandiosity (Cain, Pincus, & Ansell, 2008; Lannin, Guyll, Krizan, Madon, & Cornish, 2014). Vulnerability refers to feelings of inadequacy and negative emotionality, although it is also characterized by entitlement and grandiose fantasy that can be defined as almost irrational. On the other side, grandiosity refers to interpersonal dominance, need for attention, and demonstration of entitlement, which result in a lack of empathy and decision-making driven by self-consideration and ignoring different views. When the conditions of vulnerability and grandiosity are threatened, narcissists tend to become arrogant and angry – they respond in an exaggerated and hostile way; amoral – they may commit acts of cruelty to reach their goals; and paranoid – they are suspicious of supporters and others close to them. All these characteristics complicate and endanger social relationships.

According to Maccoby (2003), the destructive side of narcissistic entrepreneurs leads to some negative behaviors that impact on the harmony of the firm. Because they are sensitive to criticism, they have difficulties communicating their emotions and sometimes their ideas.

This behavior impacts on their relationship with peers and employees who, to avoid competition, become unable and unwilling to freely express their dissent. Narcissists prefer an army of yes-persons. Their inability to listen is linked to their sensitivity to criticism. They avoid listening to others to protect themselves from criticism when they are interacting with people they cannot mistreat. Narcissists think they do not need to listen to different perceptions since they have reached their current position with no one's help. Moreover, they reject the importance of educational or mentoring programs because they think they are not important to being successful. Similarly, they avoid taking on a mentoring role because they feel superior and they cannot waste their time on useless things. However, if they decide to take on this role, they tend to mentor only younger people or individuals they consider inferior. Narcissistic entrepreneurs have a strong desire to compete; they become merciless and harsh to achieve their goals, without limiting their behaviors or using awareness and sensitivity. This competition reflects on employees' behavior – they too develop strong internal competitiveness that causes battles and enmity.

2.6.2 The Positive Side of Entrepreneurial Narcissism

On the other hand, narcissists can be productive/constructive. They are people who have a precise vision about how to change the world and pursue that vision with passion and perseverance, who act independently, who have strategic intelligence and are charismatic, risk-takers, and competitive.

Narcissists see the world as a place that needs to be changed; if their plans fail, they are able to mobilize their strengths to achieve their goals. Narcissistic entrepreneurs use their firms as vehicles to enforce these changes (Baum & Locke, 2004; Goncalo, Flynn, & Kim, 2010; Maccoby, 2000). Passion and perseverance allow them to take this idea of change forward. In fact, productive narcissists constantly have new ideas, and when they find their purpose, their passion develops. Sometimes peers are overwhelmed by the narcissist's creative flow and some of them are tormented by persistent phone calls, in which narcissists list their new ideas, ask for opinions but do not listen to the answers (Goncalo et al., 2010; Maccoby, 2003). Moreover, perseverance allows productive narcissists to be undiscouraged by failure. Productive narcissists are resilient; they learn from failure and bounce back (Maccoby, 2000). "For the passionate productive narcissist, there is no such thing as personal life, because their work is their life; changing the world is not something that happens during office hours" (Maccoby, 2003, p. 116).

Productive narcissists have independent thinking, that is, they are free from internal and external constraints. Freedom from internal constraints is linked to freedom of thought because narcissistic entrepreneurs do not pay attention to the social pressure that would lead them to conform, while freedom from external constraints is related to their freedom to act as they wish because they are not imprisoned by a fixed schema (Lakey, Rose, Campbell, & Goodie, 2008).

Strategic intelligence enables productive narcissists to stay in power and sustain success, even if there are losses (Maccoby, 2012; Maccoby & Scudder, 2011). The four qualities included in strategic intelligence are: foresight, visioning with system thinking, partnering, and motivating and empowering. Foresight refers to the ability to anticipate how current movements, ideas, and forces will play out in the future, which drives productive narcissists to understand and predict sudden changes in technology, products, competitors, and customers' needs and values. Visioning with system thinking means that productive narcissists have an unusual way of seeing the world – they are able to synthesize and integrate all the information they have instead of treating it as separate pieces of data. Partnering means making strategic alliances to achieve predetermined goals. Motivating and empowering mean the ability to get people to embrace a common purpose and implement the entrepreneur's vision.

Finally, productive narcissists are charismatic, risk-takers, and competitive. Charisma derives from the productive narcissist's ability to easily charm and motivate people, leading to their admiration. Admiration due to their use of the art of rhetoric to persuade, influence, and mobilize others creates spontaneity and self-confidence in narcissistic entrepreneurs (Gardner & Avolio, 1998; Goncalo et al., 2010; Maccoby, 2003). Moreover, productive narcissists are willing to take risks that others dare not take because they are able to create and seize opportunities (Lakey et al., 2008). Finally, narcissistic entrepreneurs are driven by an overwhelming desire to compete, and this leads them to undertake bolder and more aggressive strategic actions (Lumpkin & Dess, 1996; Maccoby, 2000; Rosenthal & Pittinsky, 2006).

Table 2.2 summarizes the main characteristics of productive narcissists, as described in the literature.

Table 2.2   *The main adjectives describing productive narcissists in the literature*

Adjective	Description	Authors
Vision of changing the world	They see the world as a place that needs change They use firms as vehicles for their visions	Baum and Locke (2004); Goncalo et al. (2010); Maccoby (2000)
Passion	They are curious They constantly have new ideas that need to be tested and tried out	Goncalo et al. (2010); Maccoby (2003)
Perseverance	They are not discouraged by failure They use failures to improve their knowledge	Maccoby (2000)
Independent thinking	They are free from internal constraints (e.g., social pressure) and external constraints (act as they wish and believe)	Maccoby (2000)
Strategic intelligence — Foresight	They are able to anticipate how current movements, ideas, and forces will play out in the future, driving changes in technology, products, competitors, and customers' needs and values	Maccoby (2012); Maccoby and Scudder (2011)
Strategic intelligence — Visioning with system thinking	They are able to synthesize and integrate all the information they have, instead of treating it as separate pieces of data	
Strategic intelligence — Partnering	They make strategic alliances to achieve goals	
Strategic intelligence — Motivating and empowering	They are able to get people to embrace a common purpose and implement their vision	
Charisma	They employ the art of rhetoric to persuade, influence, and mobilize others; if they know they are admired by others, they become more spontaneous and more certain of their message	Gardner and Avolio (1998); Goncalo et al. (2010); Maccoby (2003)

Adjective	Description	Authors
Risk-taking	They take risks that others cannot or dare not They are able to create and seize opportunities	Lakey et al. (2008)
Competitiveness	They prefer to take bolder and more aggressive strategic actions	Lumpkin and Dess (1996); Maccoby (2000); Rosenthal and Pittinsky (2006)

Source: Our elaboration.

2.7   ENTREPRENEUR NARCISSISM AND SMALL FIRM PERFORMANCE

In recent years, researchers have paid a lot of attention to the study of entrepreneur narcissism and the way it impacts on the various phases of entrepreneurial life, that is, business creation, strategic management, and performance evaluation.

Regarding the business idea and business creation, entrepreneur narcissism is positively related to entrepreneurial intentions because individuals with high narcissistic tendencies are more risk prone (Hmieleski & Lerner, 2016; Mathieu & St-Jean, 2013). Other studies found that a high level of narcissism offers numerous advantages in starting new ventures since it involves innovativeness, risk-taking, need for achievement, and self-confidence, typical characteristics of narcissistic entrepreneurs (Do & Dadvari, 2017; Hayward, Forster, Sarasvathy, & Fredrickson, 2010). Finally, narcissistic individuals can pursue an entrepreneurial path to satisfy their need for self-enhancement and adoration. In fact, CEOs and entrepreneurs generally show higher levels of narcissism compared to other people (Navis & Ozbek, 2016).

With reference to firm strategic management, in many cases, narcissistic entrepreneurs use their firms to satisfy their desires and preferences (Maccoby, 2000). They have compelling visions for firms (Goncalo et al., 2010; Maccoby, 2012), and for this reason, instead of creating a balanced, permanent, and strong strategic environment, they are likely to push towards an environment characterized by a search for exaltation and distinction (Byrne & Worthy, 2013). The prevailing motto of narcissistic entrepreneurs is: "I do not try to understand the future because I will create it". Moreover, due to their need to emerge, be seen and admired, narcissistic entrepreneurs have a tendency to enter into transactions that rapidly change the dynamics of the firm and increase its visibility (Judge, LePine, & Rich, 2006). They tend to dissociate themselves from maintaining the status quo and have a propensity to deviate from stale, previous, strategies (Chatterjee & Hambrick, 2007). Finally, narcissistic entrepreneurs undertake actions that are overly risky and overly reward-ing at the same time (Foster, Misra, & Reidy, 2009; Foster & Trimm, 2008). Moreover, in addition to the desire for emergence, they tend to overvalue their ability while underestimating the risk of failure (Judge et al., 2006). For example, they generally prefer to create unconventional products that could reap a lot of benefits, but also deep losses, thus pre-ferring to implement radical more than incremental innovation (Galasso & Simcoe, 2011; Zhang, Ou, Tsui, & Wang, 2017).

Regarding firms' performance, various studies suggest that entre-preneur narcissism can be deleterious since it leads entrepreneurs to take undue risk (Chatterjee & Hambrick, 2007) and not be aware of objective performance indicators (Chatterjee & Hambrick, 2011). On the other hand, others underline that narcissism has also a positive side that positively affects business performance (Judge et al., 2009; Lubit, 2002; Rosenthal & Pittinsky, 2006; Wales et al., 2013), especially in times of crisis (Patel & Cooper, 2014). With reference to research find-ings, Chatterjee and Hambrick (2007) observe that narcissists typically generate more extreme and irregular performance than non-narcissists but, ultimately, narcissists do not systematically generate better or worse performance. Chatterjee and Hambrick (2011) suggest that the positive relationship between social praise and risk-taking is stronger in narcissistic individuals than less narcissistic individuals. Despite this, narcissism does not appear to be related to acquisition premium or risky outlays. In the analysis carried out by Resick, Whitman, Weingarden, and Hiller (2009) entrepreneur narcissism and firm performance are not significantly correlated. Wales et al. (2013), on the other hand, detect the existence of a positive relationship between entrepreneur narcissism and firm performance, as well as a partial mediation effect of entre-preneurial orientation. Patel and Cooper (2014) distinguish between two different periods: crisis periods, where narcissistic entrepreneurs suffer from greater declines in performance, and post-crisis periods, where greater performance gains are experienced. In Reina, Zhang, and Peterson (2014), entrepreneurs' narcissism has several implications in group dynamics and performance in firms – narcissism exhibits either beneficial or detrimental effects, depending on the entrepreneur's level of "oneness" with his or her organization.

REFERENCES

Abebe, M., & Alvarado, D. A. (2013). Founder–CEO status and firm performance: An exploratory study of alternative perspectives. *Journal of Strategy and Management, 6*(4), 343–357.

Ackerman, R. A., Witt, E. A., Donnellan, M. B., Trzesniewski, K. H., Robins, R. W., & Kashy, D. A. (2011). What does the narcissistic personality inventory really measure? *Assessment, 18*(1), 67–87.

Agarwal, S., & Srivastava, S. (2016). Impact of locus of control on organizational role stress and job satisfaction relationship of public and private sector managerial level personnel. *Journal of Organization and Human Behaviour, 5*(3), 7–13.

Ahlin, B., Drnovšek, M., & Hisrich, R. D. (2014). Entrepreneurs' creativity and firm innovation: The moderating role of entrepreneurial self-efficacy. *Small Business Economics, 43*(1), 101–117.

Akhtar, R., Ahmetoglu, G., & Chamorro-Premuzic, T. (2013). Greed is good? Assessing the relationship between entrepreneurship and subclinical psychopathy. *Personality and Individual Differences, 54*(3), 420–425.

Alam, S. S. (2011). Entrepreneurs' traits and firm innovation capability: An empirical study in Malaysia. *Asian Journal of Technology Innovation, 19*(1), 53–66.

Ardichvili, A., Cardozo, R., & Ray, S. (2003). A theory of entrepreneurial opportunity identification and development. *Journal of Business Venturing, 18*(1), 105–123.

Asante, E. A., & Affum-Osei, E. (2019). Entrepreneurship as a career choice: The impact of locus of control on aspiring entrepreneurs' opportunity recognition. *Journal of Business Research, 98*, 227–235.

Baum, J. R., & Locke, E. A. (2004). The relationship of entrepreneurial traits, skill, and motivation to subsequent venture growth. *Journal of Applied Psychology, 89*(4), 587–598.

Bertl, B., Pietschnig, J., Tran, U. S., Stieger, S., & Voracek, M. (2017). More or less than the sum of its parts? Mapping the Dark Triad of personality onto a single Dark Core. *Personality and Individual Differences, 114*(1), 140–144.

Bird, B. (1988). Implementing entrepreneurial ideas: The case for intention. *Academy of Management Review, 13*(3), 442–453.

Boddy, C. R. (2006). The dark side of management decisions: Organisational psychopaths. *Management Decision, 44*(10), 1461–1475.

Boddy, C. R. (2015). Organisational psychopaths: A ten year update. *Management Decision, 53*(10), 2407–2432.

Boone, C., Brabander, B., & Witteloostuijn, A. (1996). CEO locus of control and small firm performance: An integrative framework and empirical test. *Journal of Management Studies, 33*(5), 667–700.

Brandstätter, H. (2011). Personality aspects of entrepreneurship: A look at five meta-analyses. *Personality and Individual Differences, 51*(3), 222–230.

Brody, N. (2013). *Personality in Search of Individuality.* San Diego, CA: Academic Press.

Buckels, E. E., Jones, D. N., & Paulhus, D. L. (2013). Behavioral confirmation of everyday sadism. *Psychological Science, 24*(11), 2201–2209.

Buss, D. M. (1991). Evolutionary personality psychology. *Annual Review of Psychology, 42*(1), 459–491.

Byrne, K. A., & Worthy, D. A. (2013). Do narcissists make better decisions? An investigation of narcissism and dynamic decision-making performance. *Personality and Individual Differences, 55*(2), 112–117.

Cain, N. M., Pincus, A. L., & Ansell, E. B. (2008). Narcissism at the crossroads: Phenotypic description of pathological narcissism across clinical theory, social/personality psychology, and psychiatric diagnosis. *Clinical Psychology Review, 28*(4), 638–656.

Campbell, W. K., Goodie, A. S., & Foster, J. D. (2004). Narcissism, confidence, and risk attitude. *Journal of Behavioral Decision Making, 17*(4), 297–311.

Carland, J. W., Hoy, F., Boulton, W. R., & Carland, J. A. C. (2007). Differentiating entrepreneurs from small business owners: A conceptualization. In A. Cuervo, D. Ribeiro, & S. Roig (Eds.), *Entrepreneurship* (pp. 73–81). Heidelberg/ Berlin: Springer.

Carland, J. W., Hoy, F., & Carland, J. A. C. (1988). "Who is an entrepreneur?" Is a question worth asking. *American Journal of Small Business, 12*(4), 33–39.

Chatterjee, A., & Hambrick, D. C. (2007). It's all about me: Narcissistic chief executive officers and their effects on company strategy and performance. *Administrative Science Quarterly, 52*(3), 351–386.

Chatterjee, A., & Hambrick, D. C. (2011). Executive personality, capability cues, and risk taking: How narcissistic CEOs react to their successes and stumbles. *Administrative Science Quarterly, 56*(2), 202–237.

Choe, K.-L., Loo, S.-C., & Lau, T.-C. (2013). Exploratory study on the relationship between entrepreneurial attitude and firm's performance. *Asian Social Science, 9*(4). Retrieved from https://doi.org/10.5539/ass.v9n4p144

Christie, R., & Geis, F. L. (1970). *Studies in Machiavellianism*. San Diego, CA: Academic Press.

Church, A. T., & Lonner, W. J. (1998). The cross-cultural perspective in the study of personality: Rationale and current research. *Journal of Cross-Cultural Psychology, 29*(1), 32–62.

Ciavarella, M. A., Buchholtz, A. K., Riordan, C. M., Gatewood, R. D., & Stokes, G. S. (2004). The Big Five and venture survival: Is there a linkage? *Journal of Business Venturing, 19*(4), 465–483.

Cobb-Clark, D. A., & Schurer, S. (2012). The stability of Big-Five personality traits. *Economics Letters, 115*(1), 11–15.

Costa, P. T., & McCrae, R. R. (1976). Age differences in personality structure: A cluster analytic approach. *Journal of Gerontology, 31*(5), 564–570.

Costa, P. T., & McCrae, R. R. (1985). *The NEO Personality Inventory*. Odessa, FL: Psychological Assessment Resources.

Costa, P. T., & McCrae, R. R. (1992). Normal personality assessment in clinical practice: The NEO Personality Inventory. *Psychological Assessment, 4*(1), 5–13.

Côté, S., DeCelles, K. A., McCarthy, J. M., Van Kleef, G. A., & Hideg, I. (2011). The Jekyll and Hyde of emotional intelligence: Emotion-regulation knowledge facilitates both prosocial and interpersonally deviant behavior. *Psychological Science*, *22*(8), 1073–1080.

Crysel, L. C., Crosier, B. S., & Webster, G. D. (2013). The Dark Triad and risk behavior. *Personality and Individual Differences*, *54*(1), 35–40.

Dahling, J. J., Whitaker, B. G., & Levy, P. E. (2009). The development and validation of a new Machiavellianism scale. *Journal of Management*, *35*(2), 219–257.

Dean, T. J., & McMullen, J. S. (2007). Toward a theory of sustainable entrepreneurship: Reducing environmental degradation through entrepreneurial action. *Journal of Business Venturing*, *22*(1), 50–76.

DeTienne, D. R. (2010). Entrepreneurial exit as a critical component of the entrepreneurial process: Theoretical development. *Journal of Business Venturing*, *25*(2), 203–215.

Deutschman, A. (2005). Is your boss a psychopath? *Fast Company*, **86**, 44. Retrieved from https://www.fastcompany.com/53247/your-boss-psychopath

de Vries, M. F. K. (1994). The leadership mystique. *The Academy of Management Executive*, *8*(3), 73–89.

Do, B.-R., & Dadvari, A. (2017). The influence of the Dark Triad on the relationship between entrepreneurial attitude orientation and entrepreneurial intention: A study among students in Taiwan University. *Asia Pacific Management Review*, *22*(4), 185–191.

Donnellan, M. B., & Lucas, R. E. (2008). Age differences in the Big Five across the life span: Evidence from two national samples. *Psychology and Aging*, *23*(3), 558–566.

Ellis, H. (1898). Auto-eroticism: A psychological study. *Alienist and Neurologist*, *19*, 260–299.

Emmons, R. A. (1987). Narcissism: Theory and measurement. *Journal of Personality and Social Psychology*, *52*(1), 11–17.

Fehr, B., Samsom, D., & Paulhus, D. L. (1992). The construct of Machiavellianism: Twenty years later. In C. D. Spielberger & J. N. Butcher (Eds.), *Advances in Personality Assessment* (Vol. 9, pp. 77–116). New York, NY: Routledge.

Foster, J. D., Misra, T. A., & Reidy, D. E. (2009). Narcissists are approach-oriented toward their money and their friends. *Journal of Research in Personality*, *43*(5), 764–769.

Foster, J. D., & Trimm, R. F. (2008). On being eager and uninhibited: Narcissism and approach–avoidance motivation. *Personality and Social Psychology Bulletin*, *34*(7), 1004–1017.

Freud, S. (1914 [1991]). On narcissism: An introduction. In J. Sandler, E. Spector Person, & P. Fonagy (Eds.), *Freud's "On narcissism: An introduction"* (standard ed., pp. 3–32). New Haven, CT: Yale University Press.

Furnham, A., Richards, S. C., & Paulhus, D. L. (2013). The Dark Triad of personality: A 10 year review. *Social and Personality Psychology Compass*, *7*(3), 199–216.

Galasso, A., & Simcoe, T. S. (2011). CEO overconfidence and innovation. *Management Science*, *57*(8), 1469–1484.

Galvin, B. M., Randel, A. E., Collins, B. J., & Johnson, R. E. (2018). Changing the focus of locus (of control): A targeted review of the locus of control literature and agenda for future research. *Journal of Organizational Behavior, 39*(7), 820–833.

Gardner, W. L., & Avolio, B. J. (1998). The charismatic relationship: A dramaturgical perspective. *Academy of Management Review, 23*(1), 32–58.

Gartner, W. B. (1985). A conceptual framework for describing the phenomenon of new venture creation. *Academy of Management Review, 10*(4), 696–706.

Gartner, W. B. (1988). "Who is an entrepreneur?" Is the wrong question. *American Journal of Small Business, 12*(4), 11–32.

Gartner, W. B. (1990). What are we talking about when we talk about entrepreneurship? *Journal of Business Venturing, 5*(1), 15–28.

Gartner, W. B. (2001). Is there an elephant in entrepreneurship? Blind assumptions in theory development. *Entrepreneurship Theory and Practice, 25*(4), 27–39.

Gatewood, E. J., Shaver, K. G., & Gartner, W. B. (1995). A longitudinal study of cognitive factors influencing start-up behaviors and success at venture creation. *Journal of Business Venturing, 10*(5), 371–391.

Goldberg, L. (1983). *The magical number five, plus or minus two: Some considerations on the dimensionality of personality descriptors* [Paper presentation]. Research Seminar, Gerontology Research Center, Baltimore, MD, USA.

Goncalo, J.A., Flynn, F. J., & Kim, S. H. (2010). Are two narcissists better than one? The link between narcissism, perceived creativity, and creative performance. *Personality and Social Psychology Bulletin, 36*(11), 1484–1495.

Goodstadt, B. E., & Hjelle, L. A. (1973). Power to the powerless: Locus of control and the use of power. *Journal of Personality and Social Psychology, 27*(2), 190–196.

Gunawan, A., & Munari, M. (2019). The association between locus of control and job satisfaction to auditor ethical sensitivity. *Journal of Accounting and Strategic Finance, 2*(2), 193–207.

Hafeez, M. H., Shariff, M. N. M., & Lazim, H. B. M. (2012). Relationship between entrepreneurial orientation, firm resources, SME branding and firm's performance: Is innovation the missing link? *American Journal of Industrial and Business Management, 2*(4), 153–159.

Hambrick, D. C., & Mason, P. A. (1984). Upper echelons: The organization as a reflection of its top managers. *Academy of Management Review, 9*(2), 193–206.

Hansen, D. J., Shrader, R., & Monllor, J. (2011). Defragmenting definitions of entrepreneurial opportunity. *Journal of Small Business Management, 49*(2), 283–304.

Hare, R. D. (1999). *Without conscience: The disturbing world of the psychopaths among us*. New York, NY: Guilford Press.

Hayward, M. L., Forster, W. R., Sarasvathy, S. D., & Fredrickson, B. L. (2010). Beyond hubris: How highly confident entrepreneurs rebound to venture again. *Journal of Business Venturing, 25*(6), 569–578.

He, L. (2008). Do founders matter? A study of executive compensation, governance structure and firm performance. *Journal of Business Venturing, 23*(3), 257–279.

Hmieleski, K. M., & Lerner, D. A. (2016). The Dark Triad and nascent entrepreneurship: An examination of unproductive versus productive entrepreneurial motives. *Journal of Small Business Management, 54*, 7–32.

Howell, J. M., & Avolio, B. J. (1993). Transformational leadership, transactional leadership, locus of control, and support for innovation: Key predictors of consolidated-business-unit performance. *Journal of Applied Psychology, 78*(6), 891–902.

Hsiao, C., Lee, Y.-H., & Chen, H.-H. (2016). The effects of internal locus of control on entrepreneurship: The mediating mechanisms of social capital and human capital. *The International Journal of Human Resource Management, 27*(11), 1158–1172.

Huefner, J. C., & Hunt, H. K. (1994). Broadening the concept of entrepreneurship: Comparing business and consumer entrepreneurs. *Entrepreneurship Theory and Practice, 18*(3), 61–75.

Humphreys, J. H., Haden, S. P., Novicevic, M. M., Clayton, R. W., & Gibson, J. W. (2011). Lillian McMurry of Trumpet Records: Integrity and authenticity in the charismatic, constructive narcissist leader. *Journal of Leadership and Organizational Studies, 18*(1), 40–55.

Hutter, K., Füller, J., Hautz, J., Bilgram, V., & Matzler, K. (2015). Machiavellianism or morality: Which behavior pays off in online innovation contests? *Journal of Management Information Systems, 32*(3), 197–228.

John, O. P., & Srivastava, S. (1999). The Big Five trait taxonomy: History, measurement, and theoretical perspectives. In L. A. Pervin & O. P. John (Eds.), *Handbook of personality: Theory and research* (2nd ed., pp. 102–138). New York, NY: Guilford Press.

Jonason, P. K., & Krause, L. (2013). The emotional deficits associated with the Dark Triad traits: Cognitive empathy, affective empathy, and alexithymia. *Personality and Individual Differences, 55*(5), 532–537.

Jonason, P. K., Li, N. P., & Teicher, E. A. (2010). Who is James Bond? The Dark Triad as an agentic social style. *Individual Differences Research, 8*(2), 111–120.

Jones, D. N., & Figueredo, A. J. (2013). The core of darkness: Uncovering the heart of the Dark Triad. *European Journal of Personality, 27*(6), 521–531.

Judge, T. A., & Bono, J. E. (2000). Five-factor model of personality and transformational leadership. *Journal of Applied Psychology, 85*(5), 751–765.

Judge, T. A., & LePine, J. A. (2007). The bright and dark sides of personality: Implications for personnel selection in individual and team contexts. In J. Legan-Fox & R. J. Klimoski (Eds.), *Research companion to the dysfunctional workplace: Management challenges and symptoms* (pp. 332–355). Cheltenham, UK and Northampton, MA, USA: Edward Elgar Publishing.

Judge, T. A., LePine, J. A., & Rich, B. L. (2006). Loving yourself abundantly: Relationship of the narcissistic personality to self- and other perceptions of workplace deviance, leadership, and task and contextual performance. *Journal of Applied Psychology, 91*(4), 762–776.

Judge, T. A., Piccolo, R. F., & Kosalka, T. (2009). The bright and dark sides of leader traits: A review and theoretical extension of the leader trait paradigm. *The Leadership Quarterly, 20*(6), 855–875.

Kang, J. H., Solomon, G. T., & Choi, D. Y. (2015). CEOs' leadership styles and managers' innovative behaviour: Investigation of intervening effects in an entrepreneurial context. *Journal of Management Studies, 52*(4), 531–554.

Kickul, J., & Gundry, L. (2002). Prospecting for strategic advantage: The proactive entrepreneurial personality and small firm innovation. *Journal of Small Business Management, 40*(2), 85–97.

Kickul, J., & Walters, J. (2002). Recognizing new opportunities and innovations: The role of strategic orientation and proactivity in Internet firms. *International Journal of Entrepreneurial Behavior & Research, 8*(6), 292–308.

Kimmons, G., & Greenhaus, J. H. (1976). Relationship between locus of control and reactions of employees to work characteristics. *Psychological Reports, 39*(3), 815–820.

Klein, P. G. (2008). Opportunity discovery, entrepreneurial action, and economic organization. *Strategic Entrepreneurship Journal, 2*(3), 175–190.

Klotz, A. C., & Neubaum, D. O. (2016). Research on the dark side of personality traits in entrepreneurship: Observations from an organizational behavior perspective. *Entrepreneurship Theory and Practice, 40*(1), 7–17.

Kramer, M., Cesinger, B., Schwarzinger, D., & Gelléri, P. (2011). *Entrepreneurship and the Dark Triad of personality: How narcissism, Machiavellianism, and psychopathy relate to entrepreneurial intention and performance* [Paper presentation]. 6th European Conference on Innovation and Entrepreneurship, Aberdeen, UK.

Lakey, C. E., Rose, P., Campbell, W. K., & Goodie, A. S. (2008). Probing the link between narcissism and gambling: The mediating role of judgment and decision-making biases. *Journal of Behavioral Decision Making, 21*(2), 113–137.

Lannin, D. G., Guyll, M., Krizan, Z., Madon, S., & Cornish, M. (2014). When are grandiose and vulnerable narcissists least helpful? *Personality and Individual Differences, 56*, 127–132.

Lee, D. Y., & Tsang, E. W. (2001). The effects of entrepreneurial personality, background and network activities on venture growth. *Journal of Management Studies, 38*(4), 583–602.

Leonelli, S., Ceci, F., & Masciarelli, F. (2016). The importance of entrepreneurs' traits in explaining start-ups' innovativeness. *Sinergie: Italian Journal of Management, 34*(101), 71–85.

Leonelli, S., Masciarelli, F., & Fontana, F. (2019). The impact of personality traits and abilities on entrepreneurial orientation in SMEs. *Journal of Small Business & Entrepreneurship*. Retrieved from https://doi.org/10.1080/08276331.2019.166633933

Littunen, H. (2000). Entrepreneurship and the characteristics of the entrepreneurial personality. *International Journal of Entrepreneurial Behavior & Research, 6*(6), 295–310.

Locke, E. A. (2000). *The prime movers.* New York, NY: AMACOM.

Lubit, R. (2002). The long-term organizational impact of destructively narcissistic managers. *The Academy of Management Executive, 16*(1), 127–138.

Lukeš, M. (2013). Entrepreneurs as innovators: A multi-country study on entrepreneurs' innovative behaviour. *Prague Economic Papers, 22*(1), 72–84.

Lumpkin, G. T., & Dess, G. G. (1996). Clarifying the entrepreneurial orientation construct and linking it to performance. *The Academy of Management Review, 21*(1), 135–172.

Luthans, F., Avey, J. B., Avolio, B. J., Norman, S. M., & Combs, G. M. (2006). Psychological capital development: Toward a micro-intervention. *Journal of Organizational Behavior, 27*(3), 387–393.

Maccoby, M. (2000). Narcissistic leaders: The incredible pros, the inevitable cons. *Harvard Business Review, 78*(1), 68–78.

Maccoby, M. (2003). *The productive narcissist: The promise and peril of visionary leadership.* New York, NY: Broadway Books.

Maccoby, M. (2012). *Narcissistic leaders: Who succeeds and who fails.* London: Crown Business.

Maccoby, M., & Scudder, T. (2011). Strategic intelligence: A conceptual system of leadership for change. *Performance Improvement, 50*(3), 32–40.

Machiavelli, N. (1513 [2006]). *The Prince.* Trans. W. K. Marriott. Project Gutenberg. [e-Book]. Retrieved from http://www.gutenberg.org/files/1232/1232-h/1232-h.htm

Marino, L., & Tucker, R. (2016). A dash of psychopathy may help women entrepreneurs. *Entrepreneur & Innovation Exchange.* Retrieved from https://doi.org//10.17919/X9KK5H

Mathieu, C., & St-Jean, É. (2013). Entrepreneurial personality: The role of narcissism. *Personality and Individual Differences, 55*(5), 527–531.

McCrae, R. R., & Costa, P. T. (1997). Personality trait structure as a human universal. *American Psychologist, 52*(5), 509–516.

McCrae, R. R., & Costa, P. T. (1999). A five-factor theory of personality. In L. A. Pervin & O. P. John (Eds.), *Handbook of personality: Theory and research* (2nd ed., pp. 159–181). New York, NY: Guilford Press.

McCrae, R. R., & John, O. P. (1992). An introduction to the five-factor model and its applications. *Journal of Personality, 60*(2), 175–215.

McHoskey, J. W., Worzel, W., & Szyarto, C. (1998). Machiavellianism and psychopathy. *Journal of Personality and Social Psychology, 74*(1), 192–210.

McKenzie, B., Ugbah, S. D., & Smothers, N. (2007). "Who is an entrepreneur?" Is it still the wrong question? *Academy of Entrepreneurship Journal, 13*(1), 23–43.

McMullen, J. S., & Shepherd, D. A. (2006). Entrepreneurial action and the role of uncertainty in the theory of the entrepreneur. *Academy of Management Review, 31*(1), 132–152.

Miller, D., Kets de Vries, M. F., & Toulouse, J.-M. (1982). Top executive locus of control and its relationship to strategy-making, structure, and environment. *Academy of Management Journal, 25*(2), 237–253.

Miller, D., & Toulouse, J.-M. (1986). Chief executive personality and corporate strategy and structure in small firms. *Management Science, 32*(11), 1389–1409.

Mitchell, T. R., Smyser, C. M., & Weed, S. E. (1975). Locus of control: Supervision and work satisfaction. *Academy of Management Journal, 18*(3), 623–631.

Morgan, J., & Sisak, D. (2016). Aspiring to succeed: A model of entrepreneurship and fear of failure. *Journal of Business Venturing, 31*(1), 1–21.

Mount, M. K., & Barrick, M. R. (1995). The Big Five personality dimensions: Implications for research and practice in human resources management. *Research in Personnel and Human Resources Management, 13*(3), 153–200.

Mullins-Sweatt, S. N., Glover, N. G., Derefinko, K. J., Miller, J. D., & Widiger, T. A. (2010). The search for the successful psychopath. *Journal of Research in Personality, 44*(4), 554–558.

Navis, C., & Ozbek, O. V. (2016). The right people in the wrong places: The paradox of entrepreneurial entry and successful opportunity realization. *Academy of Management Review, 41*(1), 109–129.

Nga, J. K. H., & Shamuganathan, G. (2010). The influence of personality traits and demographic factors on social entrepreneurship start up intentions. *Journal of Business Ethics, 95*(2), 259–282.

Niewiarowski, J., & Karylowski, J. J. (2015). Observable and unobservable aspects of traits in self–other comparisons. *Psychological Reports, 117*(2), 496–507.

O'Reilly, C. A., Caldwell, D. F., Chatman, J. A., & Doerr, B. (2014). The promise and problems of organizational culture: CEO personality, culture, and firm performance. *Group & Organization Management, 39*(6), 595–625.

Park, J. S. (2005). Opportunity recognition and product innovation in entrepreneurial hi-tech start-ups: A new perspective and supporting case study. *Technovation, 25*(7), 739–752.

Patel, P. C., & Cooper, D. (2014). The harder they fall, the faster they rise: Approach and avoidance focus in narcissistic CEOs. *Strategic Management Journal, 35*(10), 1528–1540.

Patrick, C., Fowles, D., & Krueger, R. (2009). Triarchic conceptualization of psychopathy: Developmental origins of disinhibition, boldness, and meanness. *Development and Psychopathology, 21*(3), 913–938.

Paulhus, D. L. (2014). Toward a taxonomy of dark personalities. *Current Directions in Psychological Science, 23*(6), 421–426.

Paulhus, D. L., & Williams, K. M. (2002). The Dark Triad of personality: Narcissism, Machiavellianism, and psychopathy. *Journal of Research in Personality, 36*(6), 556–563.

Petrides, K. V., Vernon, P. A., Schermer, J. A., & Veselka, L. (2011). Trait emotional intelligence and the Dark Triad traits of personality. *Twin Research and Human Genetics, 14*(1), 35–41.

Plummer, J. T. (2000). How personality makes a difference. *Journal of Advertising Research, 40*(6), 79–83.

Raskin, R., Novacek, J., & Hogan, R. (1991). Narcissistic self-esteem management. *Journal of Personality and Social Psychology, 60*(6), 911–918.

Rauch, A., & Frese, M. (2007). Let's put the person back into entrepreneurship research: A meta-analysis on the relationship between business owners' personality traits, business creation, and success. *European Journal of Work and Organizational Psychology, 16*(4), 353–385.

Rauch, A., & Frese, M. (2014). Born to be an entrepreneur? Revisiting the personality approach to entrepreneurship. In J. R. Baum, M. Frese, & R. A.

Baron (Eds.), *The psychology of entrepreneurship* (pp. 73–98). New York, NY: Psychology Press.

Reina, C. S., Zhang, Z., & Peterson, S. J. (2014). CEO grandiose narcissism and firm performance: The role of organizational identification. *The Leadership Quarterly, 25*(5), 958–971.

Resick, C. J., Whitman, D. S., Weingarden, S. M., & Hiller, N. J. (2009). The bright-side and the dark-side of CEO personality: Examining core self-evaluations, narcissism, transformational leadership, and strategic influence. *Journal of Applied Psychology, 94*(6), 1365–1381.

Rosenthal, S. A., & Pittinsky, T. L. (2006). Narcissistic leadership. *The Leadership Quarterly, 17*(6), 617–633.

Rotter, J. B. (1954). *Social learning and clinical psychology.* New York, NY: Prentice Hall.

Rotter, J. B. (1966). Generalized expectancies for internal versus external control of reinforcement. *Psychological Monographs: General and Applied, 80*(1), 1–28.

Sakalaki, M., Richardson, C., & Thépaut, Y. (2007). Machiavellianism and economic opportunism. *Journal of Applied Social Psychology, 37*(6), 1181–1190.

Salgado, J. F. (2002). The Big Five personality dimensions and counterproductive behaviors. *International Journal of Selection and Assessment, 10*(1–2), 117–125.

Schmitt, D. P., Realo, A., Voracek, M., & Allik, J. (2008). Why can't a man be more like a woman? Sex differences in Big Five personality traits across 55 cultures. *Journal of Personality and Social Psychology, 94*(1), 168–182.

Smith, M. B., Hill, A. D., Wallace, J. C., Recendes, T., & Judge, T. A. (2017). Upsides to dark and downsides to bright personality: A multidomain review and future research agenda. *Journal of Management, 44*(1), 191–217.

Soto, C. J., John, O. P., Gosling, S. D., & Potter, J. (2011). Age differences in personality traits from 10 to 65: Big Five domains and facets in a large cross-sectional sample. *Journal of Personality and Social Psychology, 100*(2), 330–348.

Van de Ven, A. H., Hudson, R., & Schroeder, D. M. (1984). Designing new business startups: Entrepreneurial, organizational, and ecological considerations. *Journal of Management, 10*(1), 87–108.

Venkataraman, S. (1997). The distinctive domain of entrepreneurship research. In J. Katz (Ed.), *Advances in entrepreneurship, firm emergence and growth* (Vol. 3, pp. 119–138). Greenwich, CT: JAI Press.

Vesper, K. H. (1990). *New venture strategies.* Englewood Cliffs, NJ: Prentice-Hall.

Waelder, R. (1925). The psychoses: Their mechanisms and accessibility to influence. *International Journal of Psycho-Analysis, 6*, 259–281.

Wales, W. J., Patel, P. C., & Lumpkin, G. T. (2013). In pursuit of greatness: CEO narcissism, entrepreneurial orientation, and firm performance variance. *Journal of Management Studies, 50*(6), 1041–1069.

Wang, Z., & Wang, N. (2012). Knowledge sharing, innovation and firm performance. *Expert Systems with Applications, 39*(10), 8899–8908.

Wasserman, N. (2003). Founder-CEO succession and the paradox of entrepreneurial success. *Organization Science, 14*(2), 149–172.

Widiger, T. A., & Costa, P. T. (1994). Personality and personality disorders. *Journal of Abnormal Psychology, 103*(1), 78–91.

Wilson, D. S., Near, D., & Miller, R. R. (1996). Machiavellianism: A synthesis of the evolutionary and psychological literatures. *Psychological Bulletin, 119*(2), 285–299.

Winter, S. J., Stylianou, A. C., & Giacalone, R. A. (2004). Individual differences in the acceptability of unethical information technology practices: The case of Machiavellianism and ethical ideology. *Journal of Business Ethics, 54*(3), 273–301.

Wu, W., Wang, H., Lee, H.-Y., Lin, Y.-T., & Guo, F. (2019). How Machiavellianism, psychopathy, and narcissism affect sustainable entrepreneurial orientation: The moderating effect of psychological resilience. *Frontiers in Psychology, 10.* Retrieved from https://doi.org/10.3389/fpsyg.2019.00779

Wu, W., Wang, H., Zheng, C., & Wu, Y. J. (2019). Effect of narcissism, psychopathy and Machiavellianism on entrepreneurial intention – the mediating of entrepreneurial self-efficacy. *Frontiers in Psychology, 10*, 360. Retrieved from https://doi.org/10.3389/fpsyg.2019.00360

Zettler, I., & Solga, M. (2013). Not enough of a "dark" trait? Linking Machiavellianism to job performance. *European Journal of Personality, 27*(6), 545–554.

Zhang, H., Ou, A. Y., Tsui, A. S., & Wang, H. (2017). CEO humility, narcissism and firm innovation: A paradox perspective on CEO traits. *The Leadership Quarterly, 28*, 585–604.

Zhao, H., & Seibert, S. E. (2006). The Big Five personality dimensions and entrepreneurial status: A meta-analytical review. *Journal of Applied Psychology, 91*(2), 259–271.

Zhao, H., Seibert, S. E., & Lumpkin, G. T. (2010). The relationship of personality to entrepreneurial intentions and performance: A meta-analytic review. *Journal of Management, 36*(2), 381–404.

3. Narcissism and entrepreneurial orientation (EO) in small businesses

3.1 INTRODUCTION

Entrepreneurial orientation (EO) represents a driving force behind entrepreneurial activity (Anderson, Kreiser, Kuratko, Hornsby, & Eshima, 2015; Covin & Wales, 2012); therefore, it provides an essential impulse to economic growth, innovation, and employment (Acs, Audretsch, & Feldman, 1994; Criscuolo, Gal, & Menon, 2014; Schumpeter, 1934; Wiens & Jackson, 2015).

Mintzberg (1973) and Khandwalla (1977) were the first to conduct studies on EO. In his analysis, Mintzberg (1973) defines entrepreneurial strategy-making as a managerial disposition encompassing a relentless, active search for new opportunities of growth. Khandwalla (1977, p. 22) conceives management style as the "operating set of beliefs and norms about management held by the organization's key decision makers ... [that] when translated into action, constitute the organization's strategy for survival and growth". In his view, the entrepreneurial style involves a risky and aggressive approach to the decision-making process, as opposed to a cautious, stability-oriented one.

Miller and Friesen (1982, p. 5) conceptualized firm-level entrepreneurship, maintaining that entrepreneurial firms "innovate boldly and regularly while taking considerable risks in their product-market strategies". According to Miller (1983, p. 780), EO is a simultaneous embodiment of three dimensions: innovativeness, risk-taking, and proactiveness, suggesting that, in general, a firm cannot be described as entrepreneurial when it modifies its technology or product line ("innovates", according to our terminology), led by a mere imitation of competitors and risk avoidance. Furthermore, a certain level of proactiveness is also essential. Similarly, risk-taking firms employing financial leverage in great measure are not necessarily entrepreneurial.

EO embraces the entrepreneur's intent to pursue strategies aimed at achieving innovation (e.g., an innovative intent) and commercializing an invention (e.g., being proactive) (Anderson et al., 2015; Miller & Friesen, 1982) as well as his or her inclination to promote strategic activities with uncertain outcomes (e.g., propensity to risk) (Miller, 1983), thus taking the form of a multidimensional construct.

Much of the existing research on EO is focused on the relationship between EO and firm performance (Hughes & Morgan, 2007; Wiklund & Shepherd, 2003). However, in their analysis of 51 empirical studies, Rauch, Wiklund, Lumpkin, and Frese (2009) define the EO/performance correlation as being stable to different operationalizations and cultural contexts, calling for further investigation of EO. The paucity of studies on EO antecedents appears evident to several scholars (Covin & Lumpkin, 2011; José Ruiz-Ortega, Parra-Requena, Rodrigo-Alarcón, & García-Villaverde, 2013; Wales, Gupta, & Mousa, 2011). Only a few studies, in fact, employ EO as the dependent variable (José Ruiz-Ortega et al., 2013; Kyrgidou & Spyropoulou, 2013; Leonelli, Masciarelli, & Fontana, 2019; Sciascia, Naldi, & Hunter, 2006).

In this chapter, we will look into EO antecedents by analyzing how several entrepreneurs' personality traits can be used to explain them. In small businesses, it is the entrepreneur who largely influences strategic and management decisions (Kickul & Gundry, 2002; Peterson, Smith, Martorana, & Owens, 2003). Therefore, his or her personality is likely to have a strong impact on the firm's EO.

Among the many personality traits identified in the literature, our focus is on narcissism. A narcissist is commonly defined as an arrogant, haughty, and grandiose individual, characterized by a sense of superiority and the belief they are deserving of special treatment. Narcissists are in constant need for admiration, they lack empathy, appear authoritarian, are inclined to exploit others, and ultimately tend to overestimate their abilities (Campbell, Goodie, & Foster, 2004; Chatterjee & Hambrick, 2007; Rosenthal & Pittinsky, 2006; Wales, Patel, & Lumpkin, 2013).

Following Maccoby (2003) and Leonelli et al. (2019), we assume that narcissism comprises both a productive (or bright) and an unproductive (or dark) side. The bright side is embodied by a desire to change the world, take risks, act independently, pursue a vision with passion and perseverance, and by being endowed with a strategic intelligence (Maccoby, 2003). The dark side lies in the deliberate intent and ability to manipulate others (Lubit, 2002; Maccoby, 2003). This chapter is primarily aimed at addressing the following research question: how does entrepreneur narcissism affect EO?

On an empirical level, we analyzed a sample of 140 Italian entrepreneurial small business founders. We based our models on survey and archival data, thereby providing some interesting and significant results showing that entrepreneur narcissism does indeed affect EO. Specifically, we observe that entrepreneur narcissism in its exhibitionist and manipulative expressions can have various effects on EO.

The remainder of the chapter has the following structure. First, we present a review of the existing work on EO. Second, we outline a research model and formulate some hypotheses making a connection among entrepreneur narcissism, entrepreneur resilience, and EO. Third, we discuss our methodology and findings, concluding with some implications of our results and recommendations for future research.

3.2   THE IMPACT OF NARCISSISM ON EO

The term narcissism refers to the individual's attitudes, actions, and understandings related to managing self-esteem (Chatterjee & Hambrick, 2007). Psychologists such as Emmons (1987) suggest that narcissism can be seen as a personality dimension ranging from low to high levels, and only in the presence of extreme manifestations can it be defined as a personality disorder. Pathological narcissism has been shown to have two critical dimensions: grandiose narcissism (i.e., the intent to appear helpful to others in order to enhance one's own image) and vulnerable narcissism (i.e., hypersensitivity and anger, lack of empathy, amorality, irrationality, inflexibility, and paranoia) (Lukowitsky & Pincus, 2013; Rosenthal & Pittinsky, 2006). Our main focus is on non-pathological narcissism, exhibiting vanity, urge to demonstrate superiority over others, sense of entitlement, and desire to be in the spotlight (Miller & Campbell, 2012) as its prominent observable features. Self-love, self-admiration, and the tendency to consider others as mere extensions of oneself are also part of narcissism in its non-pathological aspect (Ackerman et al., 2011). Narcissists fantasize about fame and power, they see themselves as unique, smarter, and more attractive than others (Humphreys, Haden, Novicevic, Clayton, & Gibson, 2011; Mathieu & St-Jean, 2013). They feed off attention and admiration, and they lack empathy for their peers due to an inclination not to pay close attention to others (Maccoby, 2000).

Given their convincing and compelling business visions (e.g., rather than trying to understand the future, they want to create it), narcissists tend to become leaders. Their public pronouncements make them appear charismatic in the eyes of their audience, thus enabling them to attract followers (Goncalo, Flynn, & Kim, 2010; Maccoby, 2000). With these attributes, narcissism can be seen as a good personality trait that helps to achieve major objectives.

Due to a biased consideration of themselves and overconfidence in their abilities, narcissistic entrepreneurs often lack a coherent and accurate vision of reality, which can result in hazardous actions (Shapira, 1995). Narcissistic CEOs may overestimate the outcomes of an action they consider original and more valuable compared to the alternatives. Thompson (1967) claims that in many cases, narcissistic entrepreneurs use their businesses to satisfy their desires and preferences. Thus, narcissistic CEOs make choices and devise strategies that are likely to differ from those that might be promoted by less egotistical managers. Instead of working to establish a balanced, permanent, and robust strategic environment, they tend to push for the creation of a context dominated by a desire for acclaim and distinction, as well as risky, remarkable, extreme, excessive, and oscillating performance, that is, "big wins or big losses" (Chatterjee & Hambrick, 2007).

In line with Brown, Budzek, and Tamborski (2009), in this chapter we depict the narcissistic entrepreneur as being identified by two main characteristics: the propensity to exhibitionism and the propensity to manipulation. The exhibitionist side is mainly related to the aspects of grandiosity and self-importance (Brown et al., 2009). The exhibitionism displayed by narcissistic entrepreneurs favors their engagement in risk-taking situations, bolder firm strategies, and proactiveness taken to its extreme. The narcissistic entrepreneur feels a constant anticipation for future activities, projects, and events and their possible outcomes rather than needs and other problems. The manipulative side, on the other hand, is related to the narcissistic sense of entitlement and the willingness to exploit others for personal gain (Brown et al., 2009). Manipulativeness is manifested in the narcissistic entrepreneur's craving for adoration and respect from followers and in the prioritization of his or her personal well-being over the "health" of the firm. Our main interest lies in the propensity for exhibitionism and manipulativeness, although several features of the narcissistic entrepreneur might be linked to EO strategies.

The exhibitionist narcissistic entrepreneur will be prone to become involved in hazardous situations that others might shun (Wales et al., 2013), counting on his or her ability to control the risk and exhibiting little fear of failure (Campbell et al., 2004). This kind of narcissistic entrepreneur will be certain that the threats faced by the small or medium-size enterprise (SME) can be overcome by virtue of his or her skills and talents, and that the risks are perfectly manageable and represent the only means to meaningful opportunities (Oesterle, Elosge, & Elosge, 2016). The entrepreneur's self-confidence is thus increased, leading to bold firm strategies regardless of resource limitations. The exhibitionist aspect of narcissism also contributes to the growth of the firm's proactiveness by enhancing its willingness to pursue novel possibilities through the identification of potential gains from higher-return, entrepreneurial ventures (Wales et al., 2013). The exhibitionist narcissistic entrepreneur is capable of recognizing opportunities and profiting from them; he or she pushes the firm to act and persist in order to achieve meaningful change (Maccoby, 2000). Finally, exhibitionism encourages the firm to be innovative based on the entrepreneur's passion, perseverance, and curiosity aimed at exploring and discovering innovative ideas (Goncalo et al., 2010). In particular, the exhibitionist narcissistic entrepreneur tends to welcome new directions and methods and to be more creative as compared to the non-narcissistic entrepreneur (Marcati, Guido, & Peluso, 2008), resulting in the SME being more open to new ideas and changes (Maccoby, 2003).

Therefore, exhibitionism in a narcissistic entrepreneur can lead to the implementation of risky projects, and increased proactiveness and innovativeness, thus having a positive impact on EO, while manipulativeness leads to a desire for signs of adoration and respect from followers. The latter has its roots in the ability to use interpersonal skills to control events as well as the people involved (Yuille, 2013). This manipulativeness can be a threat to the firm's risk-taking; this kind of narcissist may prefer a non-risky alternative to secure a positive result, retaining the admiration of his or her followers. In other words, the manipulative narcissistic entrepreneur's actions may be directed towards the achievement of tangible and psychological rewards from the venture, focusing on the self rather than the entrepreneurial idea or goal (Yuille, 2013). This produces negative effects on the SME's decision to favor strategic activities with uncertain outcomes. Narcissism in its manipulative expression can reduce SME proactiveness by enhancing the entrepreneur's willingness to maneuver others into pursuing new opportunities with potential gains for him- or herself rather than the firm (Back, Schmukle, & Egloff, 2010; Blair, Helland, & Walton, 2017). Ultimately, manipulative narcissism can undermine SME innovativeness for two main reasons: (1) the manipulative narcissist entrepreneur will make decisions regardless of other people's opinions (Maccoby, 2000); and (2) the manipulative narcissist entrepreneur will influence others so that their views and ideas will become similar to their own. Accordingly, groupthink is likely to emerge within the firm (Glebovskiy, 2019), thus causing a reduction in creativity and a decrease in innovativeness. Therefore, a manipulative attitude in a narcissistic entrepreneur may threaten the implementation of hazardous projects, undermine proactiveness and innovativeness, and negatively impact on EO.

Hence, we put forward the following hypotheses:

Hypothesis 1a: The exhibitionist side of entrepreneur narcissism is positively related to EO.

Hypothesis 1b: The manipulative side of entrepreneur narcissism is negatively related to EO.

3.3 EMPIRICAL STRATEGY

3.3.1 Sample and Procedure

The present study relies on a sample of Italian SMEs listed in the Italian Chamber of Commerce register. The analysis is restricted to firms within the special category of SMEs meeting the innovative criteria identified by the Italian Chamber of Commerce (e.g., the entrepreneur is the owner or licensee of a registered patent or registered software). The initial sample included 730 SMEs. We contacted some entrepreneurs via their LinkedIn profiles to outline our project and invite them to be part of it. Entrepreneurs with no LinkedIn profile were contacted via their personal email addresses. Those that agreed to participate were sent a link to the online survey. To increase the response rate, participants were told that they would receive a personalized report at the end of the study. We collected 140 completed questionnaires, with a response rate of 19.17 percent, which is higher than in other studies based on entrepreneur surveys (Block, Sandner, & Spiegel, 2013; Cardon, Gregoire, Stevens, & Patel, 2013). After excluding firms with missing values, a final sample of 114 firms was obtained. The original survey items were in English. To ensure accurate translation into Italian, a rigorous back-translation technique (Brislin, 1980) was employed. A bilingual English-Italian speaker translated the questionnaire from English into Italian, and another

Table 3.1   *Characteristics of the survey sample*

SME Characteristics	%	Entrepreneur Characteristics	%
Industry classification		Entrepreneur age	
Commerce	7.89	< 39 years old	32.46
Manufacturing	34.21	40–49 years old	42.11
Service	57.89	50–59 years old	15.78
		> 60 years old	9.65
Firm district location		Entrepreneur education	
North	42.11	High school	21.05
Center	30.70	Bachelor's degree	9.65
South/Island	27.19	Master's degree	54.39
		PhD	14.91
Firm age		Entrepreneur gender	
< 10 years old	61.40	Male	86.84
11–20 years old	23.68	Female	13.16
> 21 years old	14.92		

Note: N = 114.

bilingual speaker translated the Italian responses back into English. The final survey was administered in the Italian language between March and November 2018; three reminder emails were sent to encourage response.

Economic and financial details were gathered from Aida, a Bureau van Dijk database containing comprehensive information about firms on the Italian territory. Aida data allow research, consultation, analysis, and processing of financial information, accounts, and business details of all joint stock companies operating in Italy.

Table 3.1 presents the characteristics of the firms and entrepreneurs sampled. Most of the firms were less than ten years old, they were located in Northern or Central Italy, and they were services firms. The entrepreneurs were mainly male, aged between 40 and 49 years, with master's-level education.

3.3.2   Measures

The EO scale developed by Hughes and Morgan (2007) considering the groups of questions related to entrepreneur risk-taking propensity, innovativeness, and proactiveness was used to measure EO. All the items were gauged on a five-point Likert scale.

With regard to entrepreneur narcissism, the most widely used questionnaire is the 40-item Narcissistic Personality Inventory (NPI-40) developed by Raskin and Terry (1988). Since entrepreneurs are usually time constrained (Wallace & Baumeister, 2002), we employed a shorter version composed of 16 items (NPI-16) designed by Ames, Rose, and Anderson (2006). Gentile (2013) suggests that forced-choice responses can negatively affect the participant's experience. To avoid this, we used a five-point Likert scale. The Likert version was created by removing the non-narcissistic statement from each item; the correlation between the two versions was very high ($r = 0.97$; $p < 0.001$). NPI-16 enables us to measure both exhibitionist narcissism and manipulative narcissism. The first emphasizes the intrapersonal relationship and is concerned with a grandiose sense of self-importance, while the second focuses on the more interpersonal relationship and is concerned with the desire for signs of adoration from others (Brown et al., 2009).

Finally, in our model we use five control variables. In line with the existing literature, we controlled for individual-, firm-, and environment-level factors to minimize variances that were not directly linked to our study. At the individual level, we controlled for entrepreneur's education measured on a four-point ordinal scale (i.e., 1 = high school, 2 = bachelor's degree, 3 = master's degree, and 4 = doctoral degree), and age measured as the effective years of entrepreneurial activity (reference year 2018). Entrepreneurs with longer/higher education are likely to have access to a greater amount of resources to support their entrepreneurial ambitions, and a stronger ability to recognize opportunities and exploit them successfully (Altinay & Wang, 2011; Frank, Korunka, Lueger, & Mugler, 2005). Entrepreneur age can influence the level of aggressiveness and risk-taking, with older entrepreneurs generally being less aggressive and risk prone (Bertrand & Schoar, 2003). At the firm level, we controlled for firm age measured as the logarithm of the effective years from firm establishment (reference year 2018), firm size measured as the natural logarithm of number of employees, and cash flow (millions of euros) measured as a continuous variable. Older firms tend to have more bureaucratic cultures, making them more or less likely to be entrepreneurially oriented (Huergo & Jaumandreu, 2004). Firm size is crucial since different-sized firms may exhibit different organizational and environmental characteristics (Engelen, Neumann, & Schmidt, 2016). We controlled for cash flow since it is deemed fundamental to both the short- and long-term survival of SMEs (Uwonda & Okello, 2015). Finally, at the environmental level, we controlled for industry sector, which refers to the SME's main activity and is captured by the industry dummies at the two-digit ATECO code (classification of economic activities adopted by the Italian Institute of Statistics), and location captured by regional dummies (corresponding to the Nomenclature of Territorial Units for Statistics level 2, NUTS 2). To survive, competing industry firms require leaders endowed with a high entrepreneurial orientation (Engelen, Neumann, & Schwens, 2015). The exact geographical location of the firm may provide a cultural milieu affecting the propensity for risk and innovativeness, and the firm owner's entrepreneurial orientation (Kreiser, Marino, Dickson, & Weaver, 2010).

Table 3.2 presents the measures and sources of the control variables.

3.3.3 Model Specifications

Exploratory factor analysis (EFA) was conducted to extract the appropriate number of factors from the EO and narcissism scales. According to Osborne and Costello (2009), a screen test is an optimal tool to decide how many factors to consider. This involves examining the eigenvalue graph to identify natural curves or breakpoints in the data when the curve flattens. For the EO scale, two factors had eigenvalues of 1 or more; the first was 2.631 and the second 0.494. However, a closer examination of the scree plot reveals a noticeable slope between the first and second factors, suggesting a one-factor solution; Cronbach's alpha 0.77.

For the NPI-16 scale, the items were divided into two categories – exhibitionist narcissism and manipulative narcissism. For the first we considered items such as "I like to be the center of attention" or "I think I am a special person", while for the second we considered items such as "I find it easy to manipulate people" and "I can make anybody believe anything I want them to". Factor analysis was applied to both. The manipulative category included three items; only one factor had an eigenvalue greater than 1 (1.437), therefore just one factor was retained; Cronbach's alpha 0.64. The exhibitionist category encompassed all the remaining items; only two factors had eigenvalues of 1 or more: 4.236 and 1.424. However, due to the noticeable slope observed in the scree plot between the first and second factors, we chose a one-factor solution; Cronbach's alpha 0.85. The Appendix to this chapter reports the factor loadings of all the variables. Based on the above, we were able to build a general linear model, which is the conventional linear regression model for continuous response variables and continuous and/or categorical predictors (McCullagh & Nelder, 1989).

Table 3.2   *Control variables description*

Variable Name	Variable Type	Description	Source
Individual level			
Entrepreneur education	Ordinal variable	1 High school 2 Bachelor's degree 3 Master's degree 4 PhD	Survey
Entrepreneur age	Continuous variable	Effective years of the entrepreneur (reference year 2018).	Survey
Firm level			
Firm age	Continuous variable	Logarithm of the effective years of the firm (reference year 2018).	Aida and Italian Chamber of Commerce register
Firm size	Continuous variable	Natural logarithm of the number of employees	Aida and Italian Chamber of Commerce register
Cash flow	Continuous variable	Millions of euros	Aida and Italian Chamber of Commerce register
Environmental level			
Industry sector	Dummy variables	At the two-digit code of ATECO	Aida and Italian Chamber of Commerce register
Firm location	Dummy variables	For each region	Aida and Italian Chamber of Commerce register

3.4   RESULTS

Table 3.3 summarizes the observations, mean and standard deviations, minimum and maximum values, and degree of correlation among the variables. Multicollinearity was checked using the variance inflation factor (VIF); the values of all our variables are between 1 and 2, meaning that they are almost completely uncorrelated to one another (Hair, Ringle, & Sarstedt, 2011). Following the recommendation in Kock (2015), we checked for common method bias by verifying the inner VIF values (Podsakoff, MacKenzie, Lee, & Podsakoff, 2003; Podsakoff,

MacKenzie, & Podsakoff, 2012); the results show lack of any method bias since all the values are below 2. Finally, discriminant validity was tested using the Heterotrait–Monotrait ratio (HTMT). Since all the values are less than 0.87 we can conclude that there is discriminant validity among the variables (Henseler, Hubona, & Ray, 2016).

Table 3.4 presents the results of the general linear model. Model 1 includes only the control variables and model 2 adds the two variables related to entrepreneur narcissism. Model 2 shows that entrepreneur age has a significant negative impact on EO ($\beta = -0.024$, $p < 0.05$) displaying that increasing levels of entrepreneur age correspond to a decrease in EO. Moreover, the exhibitionist side of the narcissist entrepreneur has a significant positive impact on EO ($\beta = 0.717$, $p < 0.001$). This supports hypothesis 1a claiming that entrepreneur exhibitionism is positively related to EO; EO increases with the level of exhibitionist narcissism. Finally, manipulative narcissism has a significant negative impact on EO ($\beta = -0.575$, $p < 0.01$). This supports hypothesis 1b claiming that manipulativeness is negatively related to EO; EO decreases with increasing narcissistic manipulativeness.

3.5   DISCUSSION AND CONCLUSION

We investigated the effect that EO has on entrepreneur narcissism. EO describes the entrepreneurial firm (Anderson et al., 2015). Exhibitionistic narcissism has been shown to have a positive effect on EO: high levels of exhibitionism correspond to high levels of EO. On the other hand, manipulative narcissism was found to have a negative effect on EO: high levels of manipulation correspond to low levels of EO.

We contribute to the entrepreneurship literature on EO antecedents (Covin & Lumpkin, 2011; Lumpkin & Dess, 1996). EO can be considered as a firm-level strategy-making process used by the firm to enact organizational purpose, sustain its vision, and create competitive advantage (Covin & Slevin, 1989). Understanding the way EO is affected by entrepreneurial narcissism gives a valuable contribution to this literature.

The present study has some limitations that could represent the starting points for further research. The sample employed includes only Italian firms; therefore, it is not possible to determine whether national culture is influencing the effects of entrepreneur narcissism and resilience on EO. It would be interesting to replicate our study in different country contexts. An ideal setting would be China since it has a more collectivist culture than Western economies. High levels of collectivism might influ-

Table 3.3   *Descriptive statistics and correlation*

Variable	Mean	Std Dev.	1	2	3	4	5	6	7	8
1 EO	−0.066	0.933	1							
2 Entrepreneur narcissism (exhibitionistic)	0.023	0.898	−0.350***	1						
3 Entrepreneur narcissism (manipulative)	−0.026	0.694	−0.153	0.741***	1					
4 Entrepreneur education	2.632	0.980	−0.038	−0.120	0.005	1				
5 Entrepreneur age	45.167	9.615	0.126	0.067	−0.111	−0.038	1			
6 Firm age	11.579	6.885	−0.002	0.021	−0.056	−0.110	0.117	1		
7 Firm size	20.430	37.716	−0.1144	−0.088	−0.066	−0.206*	0.101	0.352***	1	
8 Cash flow	174.075	915.828	−0.111	−0.055	−0.080	−0.173	0.089	0.571***	0.564***	1

Note: $N = 114$. * $p < 0.05$; *** $p < 0.001$.

Table 3.4   *Results of regression analyses*

EO	Model 1		Model 2	
Control variables				
Entrepreneur education	−0.084	(0.132)	−0.143	(0.132)
Entrepreneur age	−0.021	(0.012)	−0.024*	(0.010)
Firm age	−0.305	(0.250)	−0.135	(0.213)
Firm size	−0.044	(0.107)	−0.059	(0.099)
Cash flow	−0.000	(0.000)	−0.000	(0.000)
Main effects				
Entrepreneur narcissism (exhibitionistic)			−0.717***	(0.124)
Entrepreneur narcissism (manipulative)			−0.575**	(0.193)
Constant	−0.119	(0.930)	−0.947	(0.778)
Log likelihood	−117.703		−107.327	
AIC	2.679		2.532	
BIC	−321.529		−320.817	
N	114		114	

Note: The standard error is in parentheses. *$p < 0.05$; **$p < 0.01$; ***$p < 0.001$.

ence entrepreneur personality and abilities. Ultimately, cross-sectional data were used; the study could be replicated after three or five years to investigate whether age or life events mitigate or amplify the effects of narcissism.

REFERENCES

Ackerman, R. A., Witt, E. A., Donnellan, M. B., Trzesniewski, K. H., Robins, R. W., & Kashy, D. A. (2011). What does the Narcissistic Personality Inventory really measure? *Assessment, 18*(1), 67–87.

Acs, Z. J., Audretsch, D. B., & Feldman, M. P. (1994). R&D spillovers and recipient firm size. *The Review of Economics and Statistics, 76*(2), 336–340.

Altinay, L., & Wang, C. L. (2011). The influence of an entrepreneur's socio-cultural characteristics on the entrepreneurial orientation of small firms. *Journal of Small Business and Enterprise Development, 18*(4), 673–694.

Ames, D. R., Rose, P., & Anderson, C. P. (2006). The NPI-16 as a short measure of narcissism. *Journal of Research in Personality, 40*(4), 440–450.

Anderson, B. S., Kreiser, P. M., Kuratko, D. F., Hornsby, J. S., & Eshima, Y. (2015). Reconceptualizing entrepreneurial orientation. *Strategic Management Journal, 36*(10), 1579–1596.

Back, M. D., Schmukle, S. C., & Egloff, B. (2010). Why are narcissists so charming at first sight? Decoding the narcissism–popularity link at zero acquaintance. *Journal of Personality and Social Psychology*, *98*(1), 132–145.

Bertrand, M., & Schoar, A. (2003). Managing with style: The effect of managers on firm policies. *The Quarterly Journal of Economics*, *118*(4), 1169–1208.

Blair, C. A., Helland, K., & Walton, B. (2017). Leaders behaving badly: The relationship between narcissism and unethical leadership. *Leadership & Organization Development Journal*, *38*(2), 333–346.

Block, J., Sandner, P., & Spiegel, F. (2013). How do risk attitudes differ within the group of entrepreneurs? The role of motivation and procedural utility. *Journal of Small Business Management*, *53*(1), 183–206.

Brislin, R. W. (1980). Translation and content analysis of oral and written material. In H. C. Triandis & J. W. Berry (Eds.), *Handbook of cross-cultural psychology: Methodology* (pp. 349–444). Boston, MA: Allyn & Bacon.

Brown, R. P., Budzek, K., & Tamborski, M. (2009). On the meaning and measure of narcissism. *Personality and Social Psychology Bulletin*, *35*(7), 951–964.

Campbell, W. K., Goodie, A. S., & Foster, J. D. (2004). Narcissism, confidence, and risk attitude. *Journal of Behavioral Decision Making*, *17*(4), 297–311.

Cardon, M. S., Gregoire, D. A., Stevens, C. E., & Patel, P. C. (2013). Measuring entrepreneurial passion: Conceptual foundations and scale validation. *Journal of Business Venturing*, *28*(3), 373–396.

Chatterjee, A., & Hambrick, D. C. (2007). It's all about me: Narcissistic chief executive officers and their effects on company strategy and performance. *Administrative Science Quarterly*, *52*(3), 351–386.

Covin, J. G., & Lumpkin, G. T. (2011). Entrepreneurial orientation theory and research: Reflections on a needed construct. *Entrepreneurship Theory and Practice*, *35*(5), 855–872.

Covin, J. G., & Slevin, D. P. (1989). Strategic management of small firms in hostile and benign environments. *Strategic Management Journal*, *10*(1), 75–87.

Covin, J. G., & Wales, W. J. (2012). The measurement of entrepreneurial orientation. *Entrepreneurship Theory and Practice*, *36*(4), 677–702.

Criscuolo, C., Gal, P. N., & Menon, C. (2014). The dynamics of employment growth: New evidence from 18 countries (CEP Discussion Paper No. 1274). London: London School of Economics and Political Science.

Emmons, R. A. (1987). Narcissism: Theory and measurement. *Journal of Personality and Social Psychology*, *52*(1), 11–17.

Engelen, A., Neumann, C., & Schmidt, S. (2016). Should entrepreneurially oriented firms have narcissistic CEOs? *Journal of Management*, *42*(3), 698–721.

Engelen, A., Neumann, C., & Schwens, C. (2015). "Of course I can": The effect of CEO overconfidence on entrepreneurially oriented firms. *Entrepreneurship Theory and Practice*, *39*(5), 1137–1160.

Frank, H., Korunka, C., Lueger, M., & Mugler, J. (2005). Entrepreneurial orientation and education in Austrian secondary schools: Status quo and recommendations. *Journal of Small Business and Enterprise Development*, *12*(2), 259–273.

Gentile, B. (2013). Investigating alternative response sets with the Narcissistic Personality Inventory: Validation of a new Likert version [Doctoral dissertation, University of Georgia].

Glebovskiy, A. (2019). Criminogenic isomorphism and groupthink in the business context. *International Journal of Organization Theory & Behavior, 22*(1), 22–42.

Goncalo, J. A., Flynn, F. J., & Kim, S. H. (2010). Are two narcissists better than one? The link between narcissism, perceived creativity, and creative performance. *Personality and Social Psychology Bulletin, 36*(11), 1484–1495.

Hair, J. F., Ringle, C. M., & Sarstedt, M. (2011). PLS-SEM: Indeed a silver bullet. *Journal of Marketing Theory and Practice, 19*(2), 139–152.

Henseler, J., Hubona, G., & Ray, P. A. (2016). Using PLS path modeling in new technology research: Updated guidelines. *Industrial Management & Data Systems, 116*(1), 2–20.

Huergo, E., & Jaumandreu, J. (2004). How does probability of innovation change with firm age? *Small Business Economics, 22*(3–4), 193–207.

Hughes, M., & Morgan, R. E. (2007). Deconstructing the relationship between entrepreneurial orientation and business performance at the embryonic stage of firm growth. *Industrial Marketing Management, 36*(5), 651–661.

Humphreys, J. H., Haden, S. P., Novicevic, M. M., Clayton, R. W., & Gibson, J. W. (2011). Lillian McMurry of Trumpet Records: Integrity and authenticity in the charismatic, constructive narcissist leader. *Journal of Leadership and Organizational Studies, 18*(1), 40–55.

José Ruiz-Ortega, M., Parra-Requena, G., Rodrigo-Alarcón, J., & García-Villaverde, P. M. (2013). Environmental dynamism and entrepreneurial orientation: The moderating role of firms' capabilities. *Journal of Organizational Change Management, 26*(3), 475–493.

Khandwalla, P. N. (1977). *The design of organizations.* New York, NY: Harcourt Brace Jovanovich.

Kickul, J., & Gundry, L. (2002). Prospecting for strategic advantage: The proactive entrepreneurial personality and small firm innovation. *Journal of Small Business Management, 40*(2), 85–97.

Kock, N. (2015). Common method bias in PLS-SEM: A full collinearity assessment approach. *International Journal of e-Collaboration (IJeC), 11*(4), 1–10.

Kreiser, P. M., Marino, L. D., Dickson, P., & Weaver, K. M. (2010). Cultural influences on entrepreneurial orientation: The impact of national culture on risk taking and proactiveness in SMEs. *Entrepreneurship Theory and Practice, 34*(5), 959–983.

Kyrgidou, L. P., & Spyropoulou, S. (2013). Drivers and performance outcomes of innovativeness: An empirical study. *British Journal of Management, 24*(3), 281–298.

Leonelli, S., Masciarelli, F., & Fontana, F. (2019). The impact of personality traits and abilities on entrepreneurial orientation in SMEs. *Journal of Small Business & Entrepreneurship.* Retrieved from https://doi.org/10.1080/08276331.2019.1666339

Lubit, R. (2002). The long-term organizational impact of destructively narcissistic managers. *The Academy of Management Executive, 16*(1), 127–138.

Lukowitsky, M. R., & Pincus, A. L. (2013). Interpersonal perception of pathological narcissism: A social relations analysis. *Journal of Personality Assessment, 95*(3), 261–273.

Lumpkin, G. T., & Dess, G. G. (1996). Clarifying the entrepreneurial orientation construct and linking it to performance. *The Academy of Management Review, 21*(1), 135–172.

Maccoby, M. (2000). Narcissistic leaders: The incredible pros, the inevitable cons. *Harvard Business Review, 78*(1), 68–78.

Maccoby, M. (2003). *The productive narcissist: The promise and peril of visionary leadership.* New York, NY: Broadway Books.

Marcati, A., Guido, G., & Peluso, A. M. (2008). The role of SME entrepreneurs' innovativeness and personality in the adoption of innovations. *Research Policy, 37*(9), 1579–1590.

Mathieu, C., & St-Jean, É. (2013). Entrepreneurial personality: The role of narcissism. *Personality and Individual Differences, 55*(5), 527–531.

McCullagh, P., & Nelder, J. A. (1989). *Generalized linear models.* New York, NY: Chapman & Hall/CRC.

Miller, D. (1983). The correlates of entrepreneurship in three types of firms. *Management Science, 29*(7), 770–791.

Miller, D., & Friesen, P. H. (1982). Innovation in conservative and entrepreneurial firms: Two models of strategic momentum. *Strategic Management Journal, 3*(1), 1–25.

Miller, J. D., & Campbell, W. K. (2012). Addressing criticisms of the Narcissistic Personality Inventory (NPI). In W. K. Campbell & J. D. Miller (Eds.), *The handbook of narcissism and narcissistic personality disorder: Theoretical approaches, empirical findings, and treatments* (pp. 146–152). Hoboken, NJ: John Wiley & Sons.

Mintzberg, H. (1973). Strategy-making in three modes. *California Management Review, 16*(2), 44–53.

Oesterle, M.-J., Elosge, C., & Elosge, L. (2016). Me, myself and I: The role of CEO narcissism in internationalization decisions. *International Business Review, 25*(5), 1114–1123.

Osborne, J. W., & Costello, A. B. (2009). Best practices in exploratory factor analysis: Four recommendations for getting the most from your analysis. *Pan-Pacific Management Review, 12*(2), 131–146.

Peterson, R. S., Smith, D. B., Martorana, P. V., & Owens, P. D. (2003). The impact of chief executive officer personality on top management team dynamics: One mechanism by which leadership affects organizational performance. *Journal of Applied Psychology, 88*(5), 795–808.

Podsakoff, P. M., MacKenzie, S. B., Lee, J.-Y., & Podsakoff, N. P. (2003). Common method biases in behavioral research: A critical review of the literature and recommended remedies. *Journal of Applied Psychology, 88*(5), 879–903.

Podsakoff, P. M., MacKenzie, S. B., & Podsakoff, N. P. (2012). Sources of method bias in social science research and recommendations on how to control it. *Annual Review of Psychology, 63*, 539–569.

Raskin, R., & Terry, H. (1988). A principal-components analysis of the Narcissistic Personality Inventory and further evidence of its construct validity. *Journal of Personality and Social Psychology, 54*(5), 890–902.

Rauch, A., Wiklund, J., Lumpkin, G. T., & Frese, M. (2009). Entrepreneurial orientation and business performance: An assessment of past research and suggestions for the future. *Entrepreneurship Theory and Practice, 33*(3), 761–787.

Rosenthal, S. A., & Pittinsky, T. L. (2006). Narcissistic leadership. *The Leadership Quarterly, 17*(6), 617–633.

Schumpeter, J. A. (1934). *The theory of economic development.* Cambridge, MA: Harvard University Press.

Sciascia, S., Naldi, L., & Hunter, E. (2006). Market orientation as determinant of entrepreneurship: An empirical investigation on SMEs. *The International Entrepreneurship and Management Journal, 2*(1), 21–38.

Shapira, Z. (1995). *Risk taking: A managerial perspective.* New York, NY: Russell Sage Foundation.

Thompson, E. P. (1967). Time, work-discipline, and industrial capitalism. *Past & Present,* No. 38, 56–97.

Uwonda, G., & Okello, N. (2015). Cash flow management and sustainability of small medium enterprises (SMEs) in Northern Uganda. *International Journal of Social Science and Economics Invention, 1*(03), 153–173.

Wales, W. J., Gupta, V. K., & Mousa, F.-T. (2011). Empirical research on entrepreneurial orientation: An assessment and suggestions for future research. *International Small Business Journal, 31*(4), 357–383.

Wales, W. J., Patel, P. C., & Lumpkin, G. T. (2013). In pursuit of greatness: CEO narcissism, entrepreneurial orientation, and firm performance variance. *Journal of Management Studies, 50*(6), 1041–1069.

Wallace, H. M., & Baumeister, R. F. (2002). The performance of narcissists rises and falls with perceived opportunity for glory. *Journal of Personality and Social Psychology, 82*(5), 819–834.

Wiens, J., & Jackson, C. (2015, September 25). The importance of young firms for economic growth. *Entrepreneurship Policy Digest.* Retrieved from https://www.kauffman.org/wp-content/uploads/2019/12/entrepreneurship_policy _digest_september2014.pdf

Wiklund, J., & Shepherd, D. (2003). Knowledge-based resources, entrepreneurial orientation, and the performance of small and medium-sized businesses. *Strategic Management Journal, 24*(13), 1307–1314.

Yuille, J. C. (2013). *Credibility assessment.* Amsterdam: Springer.

APPENDIX: RESULTS OF EXPLORATORY FACTOR ANALYSIS

Table A3.1   Items and factor loading EO scale

	Items	Mean	Std Dev.	Factor Loading	α
	EO scale				0.75
1	The term "risk taker" is considered a positive attribute for people in our business La propensione al rischio è un attributo positivo per le persone nella nostra azienda	3.879	1.113	0.414	
2	People in our business are encouraged to take calculated risks with new ideas Le persone nella mia azienda sono incoraggiate a calcolare i rischi derivanti dalla creazione di una nuova idea	3.836	0.964	0.420	
3	Our business emphasizes both exploration and experimentation for opportunities La mia azienda enfatizza sia l'individuazione di nuove opportunità sia la sperimentazione delle stesse	4.321	0.825	0.609	
4	We actively introduce improvements and innovations in our business Noi introduciamo spesso miglioramenti e innovazioni nella nostra azienda	4.421	0.730	0.627	
5	Our business is creative in its methods of operation La nostra attività è creativa nel modo di operare	4.193	0.936	0.645	
6	Our business seeks out new ways to do things La nostra attività è alla ricerca di nuovi metodi per fare le cose	4.329	0.909	0.638	
7	We always try to take the initiative in every situation Cerchiamo sempre di prendere l'iniziativa in ogni situazione	4.093	0.864	0.563	
8	We excel at identifying opportunities Siamo veramente bravi nell'identificare le opportunità	3.629	0.984	0.421	
9	We initiate actions to which other organizations respond Quando intraprendiamo delle azioni le altre organizzazioni ci copiano	3.429	1.106	0.449	

Source: Leonelli et al. (2019).

Table A3.2   Items and factor loading NPI-16

NPI-16	Mean	Std Dev.	Factor loading	α
				0.85
Exhibitionist side of narcissist				
1 I know that I am good because everybody keeps telling me so So che valgo perché gli altri non fanno altro che dirmelo	2.400	1.137	–*	
2 I like to be the center of attention Amo essere il centro dell'attenzione	2.388	1.135	0.764	
3 I think I am a special person Penso di essere una persona speciale	2.914	1.317	0.740	
6 I insist upon getting the respect that is due me Di solito ho il rispetto che merito	3.771	0.970	–*	
7 I am apt to show off if I get the chance Di solito cerco di essere esibizionista, se ne ho l'opportunità	1.793	0.941	0.525	
8 I always know what I am doing So sempre quello che sto facendo	3.529	1.056	–*	
9 Everybody likes to hear my stories Tutti adorano ascoltare i miei racconti	2.743	1.082	0.667	
10 I expect a great deal from other people Mi aspetto molto dalle altre persone	4.007	1.028	–*	
11 I really like to be the center of attention Mi piace molto essere al centro dell'attenzione	2.257	1.171	0.718	
12 People always seem to recognize my authority La gente riconosce sempre la mia autorità	3.371	0.962	–*	

NPI-16	Mean	Std Dev.	Factor loading	α
Exhibitionist side of narcissist				0.85
13 I am going to be a great person Diventerò una persona famosa	2.186	1.148	0.625	
15 I am more capable than other people Ho maggiori capacità rispetto alle altre persone	2.914	1.261	0.639	
16 I am an extraordinary person Sono una persona straordinaria	2.236	1.154	0.659	
Manipulative side of narcissist				0.64
4 I like having authority over people Amo avere l'autorità sugli altri	2.186	1.167	0.569	
5 I find it easy to manipulate people Trovo semplice manipolare le persone	2.914	1.261	0.772	
14 I can make anybody believe anything I want them to Posso far credere a chiunque quello che voglio	2.064	1.088	0.719	

Note: * = items excluded because factor loading is less than 0.3.
Source: Leonelli et al. (2019).

4. Exploring the relationship between entrepreneurial personality and small business innovation

4.1   INTRODUCTION

Small businesses represent the lifeblood of the economy – they have the ability to respond to changes in environmental needs, since the closeness between small business customers and managers allows these managers to easily perceive unmet customer needs (Hausman, 2005; Lonial & Carter, 2015). It is therefore crucial to understand and explain which factors influence the success of these businesses, as well as how and why they have such an impact (Coad, Segarra, & Teruel, 2016; García-Sánchez, García-Morales, & Martín-Rojas, 2018).

Cefis and Marsili (2005) suggest that innovation is important for small businesses, and owners endowed with higher operational expertise and superior customer knowledge might translate them into the creation of innovative solutions (Dahl & Moreau, 2002). Generally, innovative small businesses are those that implement product/service and process innovations (Freeman, 1995). Product/service innovations refer to the introduction of new products/services to fulfill user or external market needs. Process innovations are related to the way an organization conducts its business. The difference between innovative and non-innovative/imitative small businesses relies on the choice to implement radical vs incremental innovations. Imitative small businesses can be classified as firms with low innovative performance (Samuelsson & Davidsson, 2009), while small businesses that make incremental innovations show high innovative performance.

To improve small businesses' technological development it is essential to adopt a system for the protection of intangible assets (Levine & Sichelman, 2019). One method to protect intangible assets is patenting. Even though this kind of protection requires important investments, small and new businesses use patents to protect their ideas from competitors and to secure freedom to operate in the market (Blind, Edler, Frietsch, & Schmoch, 2006). Small firms are thereby able to profit from inventions and protect their competitive advantage (Helmers & Rogers, 2011).

Hausman (2005), using a multi-method/multi-informant process, suggests a model that shows the various factors impacting on small business innovativeness. The elements proposed are owner/manager characteristics, channel network, organizational culture, and market intensity. This chapter aims to further investigate the importance and impact of owner/manager characteristics on small firm innovation and how market intensity can moderate the above relationship.

Despite the underlined relevance of the owner/manager characteristics on firm innovativeness, prior literature has overlooked this phenomenon (Rauch & Frese, 2007) with few exceptions. Kickul and Gundry (2002) show that individuals with high strategic orientation and high abilities to identify and take opportunities have a higher propensity to develop new products or enter new markets. Zhao, Seibert, and Lumpkin (2010) demonstrate that if entrepreneurs do not have high levels of education and training in the innovative activities, they can find it difficult to transform customer needs into new products and services.

More recent literature has investigated the role of personality traits. Groenewegen and de Langen (2012) establish that risk appetite, optimism, and a logical mind are crucial to improving small business innovativeness. Song, Podoynitsyna, Van der Bij, and Halman (2008) find that openness to experience and agreeableness have a positive influence on firm innovation, while neuroticism has a negative influence. Finally, Ciavarella, Buchholtz, Riordan, Gatewood, and Stokes (2004) show that creativeness and skillfulness enable entrepreneurs to identify innovative methods to protect their firms from competition.

In this chapter, we expand previous studies related to the role of personality traits on small business innovation, aiming towards more complete knowledge of this subject. In the following sections, we will develop our research model delineating our hypotheses, and after describing the chosen method, we will present our empirical results.

4.2   THE BIG FIVE AND SMALL BUSINESS INNOVATION

The Big Five is an inclusive model of a complete set of personality traits: openness to experience, conscientiousness, extraversion, agreeableness, and neuroticism (Leonelli, Ceci, & Masciarelli, 2016). The completeness of this model allows the individual personality to be described in its entirety (McCrae & Costa, 1999), focusing on feelings and ways of thinking and behaving (Zhao & Seibert, 2006). According to numerous authors, the Big Five model is very useful to understanding entrepreneurial behavior (John & Srivastava, 1999; Rauch & Frese, 2007). As has been stated above, only a few papers have analyzed the relationship between the Big Five and small business innovation, even though personality traits are important predictors of innovative behavior. In fact, personality traits influence innovative strategies and outcomes (Hambrick & Mason, 1984), determining innovation effectiveness and efficiency within organizations. In the following subsections we will briefly illustrate each of these factors and formulate our hypotheses.

4.2.1   Openness to Experience and Small Business Innovation

Openness to experience is typical of individuals who are creative, imaginative, intelligent, and perceptive (Leonelli et al., 2016; Zhao & Seibert, 2006). First, entrepreneurs with high levels of openness to experience have high creativity levels, which helps in solving problems and finding innovative approaches (Furnham & Bachtiar, 2008). Creativity is fundamental to creating new products, discovering new business methods and applying innovative strategies (Ciavarella et al., 2004; Kornish & Ulrich, 2014; Zhao & Seibert, 2006). Second, high levels of openness to experience are related to perceptiveness and intelligence (Woo et al., 2014); these skills are essential to acquiring new knowledge and solving day-to-day problems (Zhao et al., 2010). Finally, high levels of openness to experience are associated with divergent thinking, that is, a high degree of tolerance for new ideas and new ways of doing things (Batey, Chamorro-Premuzic, & Furnham, 2009; Gal, 2019; Martindale & Dailey, 1996). Entrepreneurs with divergent thinking have the inclination and power to lead the firm to break the rules of the industry in which it competes (Zahra, 1996) and this is synonymous with radical innovation. Therefore, we put forward the following hypothesis:

Hypothesis 1 (H₁): Entrepreneur openness to experience positively affects small business innovation.

4.2.2   Conscientiousness and Small Business Innovation

Conscientiousness refers to the extent to which individuals are careful, scrupulous, and persevering. Those possessing a high level of conscientiousness are organized (i.e., they plan everything), have self-discipline (i.e., they are respectful of rules and laws), and they tend to think before acting (Leonelli et al., 2016). Moreover, they have a strong goal orientation and are ambitious, hardworking, competitive, and eager to improve and change their social standing (Papadakis & Bourantas, 1998; Zhao et al., 2010). Entrepreneurs with high levels of conscientiousness are encouraged to build new ventures and easily achieve a higher rate of productivity due to their greater efficiency and effectiveness (Baum & Locke, 2004; Ciavarella et al., 2004). Finally, to ensure long-term firm survival, they tend to invest more in innovation. Therefore, we suggest the following hypothesis:

Hypothesis 2 (H₂): Entrepreneur conscientiousness positively affects small business innovation.

4.2.3   Extraversion and Small Business Innovation

Extraversion is typical of individuals who are predisposed to positive emotional states, who feel good about themselves and the world around them (Leonelli et al., 2016). Generally, they are active, enthusiastic, and optimistic (Brandstätter, 2011); they tend to be dominant in social situations and inspire positive feelings (Rothmann & Coetzer, 2003; Zhao & Jung, 2018). Previous studies show a positive relationship between extraversion and divergent thinking (Batey et al., 2009; Chamorro-Premuzic & Reichenbacher, 2008), creative behavior (Furnham, Batey, Anand, & Manfield, 2008), and innovation in the workplace (Patterson, 2002). Entrepreneurs with high levels of extraversion are charismatic leaders (Judge & Bono, 2000; Vecchio, 2003) and able communicators. These skills help entrepreneurs transmit their ideas to peers and employees, stimulating general firm innovation. This can be made possible through the promotion of joint projects and by pushing peers and employees to share information and produce new ideas together. Extraversion may help create a "buzz" and this may then lead to innovation. Therefore, we put forward the following hypothesis:

Hypothesis 3 (H₃): Entrepreneur extraversion positively affects small business innovation.

4.2.4   Agreeableness and Small Business Innovation

Agreeableness refers to an orientation towards compassion and caring for others, and it manifests itself through the tendency to be kind, altruistic, trusting, and modest (Leonelli et al., 2016; Zhao et al., 2010). Agreeable individuals show sympathy and try to restore peace in the case of conflict (Rothmann & Coetzer, 2003). Previous studies show that agreeableness and charismatic leadership are strictly related, mainly because they have many aspects in common (De Hoogh, Den Hartog, & Koopman, 2005; de Vries, 2008). Charismatic leadership style inspires innovation since it promotes team innovation by supporting team identity and commitment, and encourages team members to cooperate through freedom of expression of ideas and participation in the decision-making process (Paulsen, Maldonado, Callan, & Ayoko, 2009). Similarly, entrepreneur agreeableness improves communication inside the firm by increasing teamworking and trust between peers and employees (Rodríguez☐Pose & Storper, 2006). These skills are important to achieving innovation since trust improves cooperation among people, so reducing coordination costs, and it allows better knowledge sharing, which increases the likelihood to innovate (Huber, 2012). For these reasons, we suggest the following hypothesis:

Hypothesis 4 (H₄): Entrepreneur agreeableness positively affects small business innovation.

4.2.5   Neuroticism and Small Business Innovation

Neuroticism is the tendency to be anxious, fearful, depressed, and moody (Leonelli et al., 2016), and it refers to the subjective inability to respond to external stimuli by keeping emotions and impulses under control (Marcati, Guido, & Peluso, 2008). Individuals with high levels of neuroticism lack self-confidence and self-esteem, and they rarely take on an entrepreneurial role (Judge & Bono, 2000; Zhao et al., 2010). This is because they neither want to take on responsibility nor be involved in risk-taking activities (Zhao & Seibert, 2006). Moreover, individuals with highly neurotic personalities find it difficult to exhibit innovative behaviors and pursue innovative ideas because of their low self-confidence and their emotional instability (Ali, 2019; Eastman, Eastman, & Tolson, 2001; Hsieh, Hsieh, & Wang, 2011). Accordingly, we propose the following hypothesis:

Hypothesis 5 (H₅): Entrepreneur neuroticism negatively affects small business innovation.

4.3 LOCUS OF CONTROL AND SMALL BUSINESS INNOVATION

Locus of control refers to the way in which individuals believe that daily life events are only influenced by their behavior (internal locus of control), or by causes beyond their control (external locus of control) (Rotter, 1954, 1966). Individuals with a strong internal locus of control are active agents of their life; therefore, they recognize that their destiny is not predetermined and they can change it (Leonelli et al., 2016). Moreover, they are conscious of their ability to influence their surroundings through their skills and efforts (Boone, Brabander, & Witteloostuijn, 1996). On the other hand, individuals characterized by an external locus of control see themselves as passive agents and believe that the events in their lives are uncontrollable due to external agents (i.e., luck, fate, powerful people or institutions) (Boone et al., 1996; Leonelli et al., 2016). By analyzing these definitions, it is clear that entrepreneurs with internal locus of control and those with external locus of control have different characteristics.

Individuals with a predominantly internal locus of control have a high likelihood of implementing an entrepreneurial career and achieving their entrepreneurial intentions (Julian & Terjesen, 2006). This is because their predisposition to act, their self-reliance, their trust in their abilities, and their willpower enable them to perceive entrepreneurial opportunities as desirable and achievable, and lead them to start a new firm (Leonelli et al., 2016). Once the firm has been established, internal locus of control can help entrepreneurs react in the event of problems. Entrepreneurs with an internal locus of control know they have high problem-solving skills; therefore, the only way to solve problems is to intervene and change the situation (Boone et al., 1996; Lefcourt, 2014). Finally, entrepreneurs with an internal locus of control may work hard to enhance firm innovation, since they are organized, proactive, and risk-takers (Miller, Kets de Vries, & Toulouse, 1982; Miller & Toulouse, 1986). In fact, entrepreneurs who feel that they have control over the destinies of their firms and environments take an active role in bringing about a change that often takes the form of innovation. Thus, we can hypothesize the following:

Hypothesis 6 (H_6): Entrepreneur internal locus of control positively affects small business innovation.

On the other hand, individuals with an external locus of control have low potential to became entrepreneurs and implement their entrepreneurial intentions because they cannot tolerate uncertainty and ambiguity (Julian & Terjesen, 2006; Miller et al., 1982). Moreover, when they find themselves facing stressful periods, they can react by feeling psychologically and physically ill (Boone et al., 1996; Lefcourt, 2014). The way entrepreneurs with an external locus of control behave is unlikely to lead to the implementation of activities involving innovation and risk-taking since they involve uncertainty and stress. Thus, we can affirm the following hypothesis:

Hypothesis 7 (H_7): Entrepreneur external locus of control negatively affects small business innovation.

4.4   DARK TRAITS AND SMALL BUSINESS INNOVATION

The Dark Triad comprises three malevolent and egocentric personality characteristics, that is, narcissism, Machiavellianism, and psychopathy. These features are generally distinguishable but sometimes have some overlapping aspects, such as the propensity to be self-serving and callous, and exploitative behavior (Jonason & Webster, 2010). Individuals high in the Dark Triad tend to be achievement oriented and skilled, and have the ability to accumulate power and extract resources from their environment (Jonason, Li, & Teicher, 2010; Jones & Figueredo, 2013). Thus, they are competitive and lack altruistic or prosocial ideals (Hmieleski & Lerner, 2016). In the following subsections we will briefly illustrate each of the factors, and we will formulate our hypotheses.

4.4.1 Narcissism and Small Business Innovation

Narcissism encompasses a broad range of entirely negative characteristics and every sort of self-absorbed and self-centered behavior (Campbell, Goodie, & Foster, 2004; Chatterjee & Hambrick, 2007). However, Maccoby (2003) gives a new perspective on narcissism, identifying a positive version called productive narcissism. Productive narcissists are risk-takers, passionate, persistent, and independent. They are driven by a desire to change the world, act independently, and pursue their strategies and visions (Maccoby, 2000). In this chapter, we will follow this new approach, considering entrepreneurs' narcissism from a productive point of view. In particular, two main characteristics of narcissistic entrepreneurs can impact on small business innovation (Leonelli et al., 2016). In the first place, their charisma helps them raise capital and extra financial input easily, which is essential to improving the innovative performance and growth of small businesses (Goncalo, Flynn, & Kim, 2010). Furthermore, charisma enables the entrepreneur to gain reassurance and support from followers, inspiring peers and employees to engage in innovative behaviors and ideas (Jung, Chow, & Wu, 2003; Keller, 2006). In the second place, narcissistic entrepreneurs have a clear vision to pursue their goal whatever the cost; these clear objectives also increase creative and innovative output from peers and employees (Sosik, Kahai, & Avolio, 1998). For these reasons, we hypothesize the following:

Hypothesis 8 (H_8): Entrepreneur narcissism positively affects small business innovation.

4.4.2 Machiavellianism and Small Business Innovation

Machiavellianism is characterized by manipulation and exploitation of others, lack of morality, and focus on self-interest (Hmieleski & Lerner, 2016). First, Machiavellian entrepreneurs (Machs) tend to manipulate and exploit peers and employees to achieve their goals. They are driven to maximize monetary gains and often use other people's suggestions and ideas, pretending they are their own, to meet their goals, without returning the favor (Hutter, Füller, Hautz, Bilgram, & Matzler, 2015). Second, Machs need immediate gratification and tend to compete aggressively (Jonason & Tost, 2010). For instance, if they have a radical and innovative idea in mind, they tend to accomplish it without considering the potential weaknesses, only focusing on the strengths and main objectives, namely competition and immediate gratification. This leads them to obfuscate or justify questionable competitive tactics and behaviors that characterize a short-term view and fast-life approach (Hmieleski & Lerner, 2016). Third, Machs can raise higher funding levels due to the positive image they put forward, their lofty aspirations, and competitive nature. As we know, extra financial inputs are essential to improving small business innovation, but Machs will invest these inputs in a cognitive analysis of the situation that will show what is the best strategy for winning rather than creating new ideas (Hutter et al., 2015; Sakalaki, Richardson, & Thépaut, 2007). Finally, Machs try to maximize their personal gain and short-term profits (Hmieleski & Lerner, 2016). They behave strategically and tactically to improve small business innovation because their main objective is to achieve a powerful position with respect to competitors. Moreover, they may invest in innovation just to satisfy a personal gain; sometimes they are not interested in the activity per se (Hutter et al., 2015). For these reasons, we put forward the following hypothesis:

Hypothesis 9 (H_9): Entrepreneur Machiavellianism positively affects small business innovation.

4.4.3   Psychopathy and Small Business Innovation

Psychopathic individuals are characterized by antisocial behavior, impulsivity, selfishness, and remorselessness (Hare, 1999). They are impulsive, which often results in risk propensity and search for continuous stimulation. In fact, their creativity is related to deviant behaviors that go against the status quo, they break the rules, and create innovation (Zibarras, Port, & Woods, 2008). However, their ability to take advantage of others (Jonason & Krause, 2013) or disregard other people's money (Jones, 2013) can lead investors not to believe in their idea and therefore not to invest in their small business, leaving them without the necessary monetary resources for investment in innovation. Finally, psychopathic entrepreneurs are poor at interpersonal relationships and tend to be shallow (Hare & Neumann, 2006). Creating good work environments and stable relationships with peers and employees favors firm innovation. Thus, we can affirm the following:

Hypothesis 10 (H$_{10}$): Entrepreneur psychopathy negatively affects small business innovation.

The research model depicted in Figure 4.1 illustrates the core components of the research and how they are related.

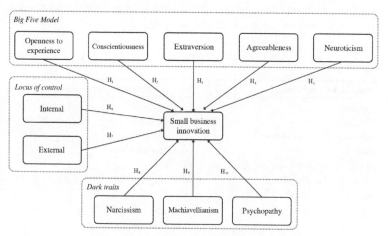

Figure 4.1   *Research model: the relationship between entrepreneurs' personality and small business innovation*

4.5   RESEARCH STRATEGY

4.5.1   Sample

The present study is of Italian small businesses and entrepreneurs. We define entrepreneurs as individuals who are the most influential members (i.e., decision-makers) in the firm, covering the role of founder, manager, and/or principal owner (Parker, 2004). We randomly selected 50 Italian small business entrepreneurs and we contacted them by email, presenting the research team and project. Meanwhile, for those registered on LinkedIn, we added them to our network to build trust and show them the authenticity of the study. In this first step, 40 entrepreneurs (80 percent) accepted our request or answered our email. After that, we sent a new email/message asking for an appointment to conduct an interview. In this second step, 35 entrepreneurs (70 percent) stated their availability.

Table 4.1 lists the main characteristics of the small businesses and entrepreneurs sampled. In particular, small firms mostly belong to the software industry, they are very small since they have between one and four employees, and they have low levels of operating capital. The majority of the entrepreneurs have master's degree level of education, are aged between 30 and 39, and are predominantly female.

Table 4.1   Characteristics of firms and entrepreneurs

Small Firm Characteristics	N	%	Entrepreneur Characteristics	N	%
Industry			*Education*		
Commerce	35	05.7	High school	35	08.6
Communication and information		05.7	Bachelor's degree		14.3
Software		51.4	Master's degree		51.4
Business administration and consulting		20.0	PhD		25.7
Research and development		02.9			
Services		14.3			
Equity			*Age*		
≤ 5000 €	33*	30.3	< 30 years old	35	17.1
5000–10 000 €		30.3	30–39 years old		40.0
10 000–50 000 €		27.3	40–49 years old		28.6
50 000–100 000 €		06.1	> 50 years old		14.3
> 100 000 €		06.0			
Employees			*Gender*		
1–4	34*	79.4	Male	35	31.4
5–9		17.7	Female		68.6
10–50		02.9			

Note: *Data not available for the whole sample.

4.5.2   Data Collection

According to King (2004), interviews are the most common method for collecting data in qualitative research. The interviews we conducted were semi-structured, with a predefined set of open-ended questions. When deemed necessary, the interviewer asked follow-up questions for in-depth answers. All 35 entrepreneurs in our sample answered the call and completed the interview. Entrepreneurs were interviewed via telephone or Skype call and the audio was recorded. They were asked for their consent at the beginning of the interviews and for each of them we recapitulated all the information about the research project.

Finally, the recorded interviews were transcribed in text form for analysis purposes. The content of the interviews was not altered in any way, although the transcripts were not phonetically precise, meaning that, for example, not all coughs or sneezes were marked down explicitly.

4.5.3   Data Analysis

We used content analysis to analyze the interviews. Content analysis is related to a series of techniques where organizationally produced content is coded to assess the meaning (McKenny, Aguinis, Short, & Anglin, 2018). This approach is a particularly valuable method for examining large volumes of text because dictionary-based procedures minimize the threat of intercoder disagreement and coder fatigue relative to manual coding (McKenny et al., 2018). We analyze each interview using the standard categories provided in the Linguistic Inquiry and Word Count (LIWC) 2015 software. This software is a text analysis program that calculates the degree to which various categories of words are used in a text, and it can process texts ranging from emails to speeches, poems, and transcribed natural language in either plain text or Word formats. The LIWC output variables we used are expressed as a percentage of total words.

Since our dependent variable is a dummy variable, we built a STATA logistic regression. We controlled for goodness of fit using STATA's command estat. The result provides support for the model used.

4.5.4   Measures

The dependent variable, *small business innovation*, was derived from the Italian patent register, and it measures a firm's propensity to patent. A dummy variable was constructed and it was given a value of one if the start-up owned at least one patent and a value of zero if it did not. It was decided to use a dummy variable because small firms generally have low numbers of patents.

The independent variables (i.e., *Big Five traits*, *locus of control*, and *dark traits*) were constructed as follows. Regarding the construction of the *Big Five traits* variables, we followed the paper by Yarkoni (2010), which validated word lists identifying several statistically significant correlations between dark traits and individual differences in word use.

Thus, considering only the relationship with a significance level higher than 99 percent ($p > 0.01$), we constructed our variables in the following way (see the Appendix at the end of the chapter for more information):

Openness to experience = – pronoun – i + article + prep – posemo – social – family – time – focuspast – focuspresent – motion – leisure – home + death

Conscientiousness = – negate – negemo – anger + achieve

Extroversion = you + social + friend + sexual

Agreeableness = we + posemo – negemo – anger + family + space + motion + leisure + home – swear

Neuroticism = – you + negemo + anx

Regarding the *locus of control* variables construction, we followed the paper by Rouhizadeh et al. (2018), which validated word lists identifying several statistically significant correlations between internal and external locus of control and words used in social network posts. Thus, considering only the relationship with a significance level higher than 99 percent ($p > 0.01$), we constructed our variables as follows (see the Appendix for more information):

Internal LOC = see + hear + interrog + relativ + auxverb + money + relig – posemo – we – shehe

External LOC = i + cogproc + sad + feel + auxverb + discrep – achieve – negemo – anx

Finally, regarding the *dark traits*, Sumner, Byers, Boochever, and Park (2012) developed and validated word lists identifying several statistically significant correlations between dark traits and personal profile online pages. In our study, considering only the relationship with a significance level higher than 95 percent ($p > 0.05$), we constructed our variables in the following way (see the Appendix for more information):

Narcissism = – dictionary words – impersonal pronouns – preposition – auxiliary verbs – conjunctions – negation – common verbs – quantifiers – anxiety + friends – discrepancy – tentative – perceptual processes + sexual – focus past – focus present + quote – apostrophes + other punctuation

Machiavellianism = − words > 6 letters − 1st person plural + negation + numbers + anger − social processes + body + swear words + fillers − dash

Psychopathy = − 1st person plural − prepositions − positive emotion + anger − family − see + body + sexual − motion − time − work + death + swear words + filler − exclaims

In our regression models, we included three control variables that might potentially affect our dependent variable. Specifically, *entrepreneur education* is measured on a four-point ordinal scale (i.e., 1 = high school, 2 = bachelor's degree, 3 = master's degree, 4 = PhD or other postgraduate certificates). *Entrepreneur age* is considered as a four-point ordinal scale (i.e., 1 = under 30 years old, 2 = 30–39 years old, 3 = 40–49 years old, and 4 = over 50 years old). Finally, we controlled for *total number of words* in the interview, as a continuous variable, to prevent the model from being influenced by the interview length.

4.6   RESULTS

Table 4.2 presents the means, standard deviations, and Spearman's correlations for all variables. Spearman's rank-order correlation is useful to measure the strength and direction of association between continuous and categorical variables. We controlled for multicollinearity using the variance inflation factor (VIF). If all the variables are completely uncorrelated with each other, both the tolerance and VIF are 1; in our case, they are close to 1.

Table 4.3 presents the findings for the logistic regressions. Model 1 only includes control variables; Model 2 adds the Big Five personality traits variables; Model 3 adds to Model 1 locus of control variables and Model 4 adds to Model 1 dark traits personality variables.

Model 1 shows no significant impact of control variables on the dependent variable. Model 2 shows that openness to experience and conscientiousness have a significant positive impact on small business innovation (β = 0.401, $p < 0.05$ and β = 2.738, $p < 0.05$ respectively), and neuroticism has a significant negative impact on small business innovation (β = −2.767, $p < 0.05$), while the last two personality traits (i.e., extraversion and agreeableness) do not have a significant impact on small business innovation. These results allow us to accept Hypothesis 1, Hypothesis 2, and Hypothesis 5, and to reject Hypothesis 3 and Hypothesis 4.

Table 4.2   *Descriptive statistics and correlation*

	Mean	Std Dev	1	2	3	4	5	6	7	8	9	10	11	12	13
1. Openness	31.304	6.431	1												
2. Conscientiousness	0.529	1.325	−0.406**	1											
3. Extraversion	12.742	2.208	0.633***	−0.076	1										
4. Agreeableness	13.129	2.336	−0.087	0.392**	0.202	1									
5. Neuroticism	0.749	0.783	0.016	0.546***	0.385**	0.289*	1								
6. Internal LOC	−21.305	2.837	0.104	0.145	0.350**	0.218	0.133	1							
7. External LOC	−24.687	3.393	0.503***	0.543***	0.033	0.598***	0.319*	0.389**	1						
8. Narcissism	167.811	6.923	−0.703***	−0.530***	0.322*	−0.336**	−0.207	−0.122	−0.676***	1					
9. Machiavellianism	−32.163	4.006	0.046	−0.115	−0.438***	−0.471***	−0.231	−0.575***	−0.390**	0.196	1				
10. Psychopathy	−33.293	2.390	0.231	−0.400**	−0.006	−0.478***	−0.197	−0.271	−0.375**	0.223	0.524***	1			
11. No. of words	1077.514	309.270	0.166	−0.003	0.137	0.133	−0.037	0.003	0.101	−0.049	0.114	0.137	1		
12. Entrepreneur education	2.943	0.873	0.010	−0.358**	0.090	0.023	−0.161	0.013	0.023	−0.153	−0.138	0.036	0.092	1	
13. Entrepreneur age	2.400	0.946	−0.023	−0.093	−0.194	−0.286*	0.117	−0.181	−0.241	0.121	0.332*	0.077	−0.153	0.054	1

Note: $N = 35$. *$p < 0.1$; **$p < 0.05$; ***$p < 0.01$.

Table 4.3   *Results of regression analyses*

DV: Small Business Innovation	Model 1	Model 2	Model 3	Model 4
Openness		0.401**		
		(0.174)		
Conscientiousness		2.738**		
		(1.160)		
Extraversion		0.285		
		(0.409)		
Agreeableness		0.024		
		(0.264)		
Neuroticism		−2.767**		
		(1.274)		
Internal LOC			2.584	
			(3.352)	
External LOC			−6.291*	
			(3.831)	
Narcissism				0.135**
				(0.070)
Machiavellianism				0.076
				(0.157)
Psychopathy				−0.479*
				(0.298)
No. of words	0.001	0.000	1.443	1.481
	(0.001)	(0.002)	(1.485)	(1.561)
Entrepreneur education	−0.211	−0.769	−0.138	−0.094
	(0.409)	(0.736)	(0.450)	(0.484)
Entrepreneur age	0.369	2.175**	0.683*	0.579*
	(0.384)	(1.049)	(0.478)	(0.465)
Constant	−1.280	−19.668**	−21.847	−48.876**
	(2.056)	(8.207)	(15.566)	(22.677)
Log likelihood	−22.917	−13.815	−20.009	−18.148
Likelihood ratio chi^2	−1.28	19.48***	7.09	10.81
Pseudo R^2	−0.027	0.414	0.151	0.230

Note: DV = dependent variable; LOC = locus of control. Standard errors are shown in parentheses. $N = 35$. *$p < 0.1$; **$p < 0.05$; ***$p < 0.01$.

Model 3 shows that external locus of control has a significant negative impact on small business innovation ($\beta = -6.291$, $p < 0.1$), while internal locus of control does not have a significant impact on small business innovation. These results allow us to accept Hypothesis 7, and to reject Hypothesis 6.

Finally, Model 4 shows that narcissism has a significant positive impact on small business innovation ($\beta = 0.135$, $p < 0.05$), psychopathy has a significant negative impact on small business innovation ($\beta = -0.479$, $p < 0.1$), while Machiavellianism does not have a significant impact on small business innovation. These results allow us to accept Hypothesis 8 and Hypothesis 10, and to reject Hypothesis 9.

Figure 4.2 summarizes the results.

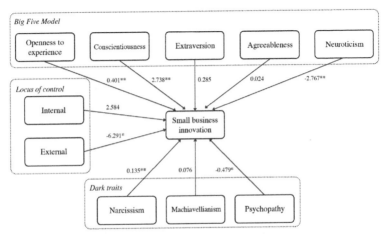

Figure 4.2   Summary results showing the impact of entrepreneurs' personality on small business innovation

4.7   DISCUSSION

The main objective of this chapter was to investigate how personality traits impact on small business innovation. Regarding the Big Five model, we have shown that openness to experience and conscientiousness have a positive impact on small business innovation, while neuroticism has a negative impact. Our findings are in line with previous studies showing that only openness, conscientiousness, and neuroticism influence innovative behavior (Gelade, 2002; Major, Turner, & Fletcher, 2006). Regarding the locus of control, we show a negative relationship between external locus of control and small business innovation. Our result is in line with Babalola's study (2009) that illustrates the importance of an internal locus of control as compared to an external locus of control regarding entrepreneurs' innovative behavior. Finally, with regard to the Dark Triad, we show that narcissism has a positive impact on small business innovation while psychopathy has a negative impact. Our results are in line with Smith and Webster's study (2018) that shows a positive relationship between grandiose narcissism (i.e., the positive side of narcissism) and employee innovation.

The relationship between entrepreneur personality and firms' performance is still understudied. Even though a limited number of papers investigate the relationship between common personality traits (i.e., Big Five) and performance, very few studies focus on the relationship between unconventional personality traits (i.e., locus of control and the Dark Triad) and performance. If we consider the relationship between personality traits and innovative performance or innovation per se, we find still fewer studies. The aim of our study is to advance the discussion on personality as a predictor of innovation, but our study only lays the foundations for a bigger stream of research that should be covered.

The present study has some limitations that suggest avenues for further research. Our results are based on a small Italian sample, therefore future studies can replicate our model but enlarging the sample and also including countries with different cultures. Furthermore, we do not consider any other effects that can mediate or moderate our relationship. It might be interesting to investigate how other personal characteristics, such as age and gender, or other relational paths, such as teamwork and networks, can influence the relationship between entrepreneur personality and small business innovation.

REFERENCES

Ali, I. (2019). Personality traits, individual innovativeness and satisfaction with life. *Journal of Innovation & Knowledge*, 4(1), 38–46.

Babalola, S. S. (2009). Women entrepreneurial innovative behaviour: The role of psychological capital. *International Journal of Business and Management*, 4(11), 184–192.

Batey, M., Chamorro-Premuzic, T., & Furnham, A. (2009). Intelligence and personality as predictors of divergent thinking: The role of general, fluid and crystallised intelligence. *Thinking Skills and Creativity*, 4(1), 60–69.

Baum, J. R., & Locke, E. A. (2004). The relationship of entrepreneurial traits, skill, and motivation to subsequent venture growth. *Journal of Applied Psychology*, 89(4), 587–598.

Blind, K., Edler, J., Frietsch, R., & Schmoch, U. (2006). Motives to patent: Empirical evidence from Germany. *Research Policy, 35*(5), 655–672.

Boone, C., Brabander, B., & Witteloostuijn, A. (1996). CEO locus of control and small firm performance: An integrative framework and empirical test. *Journal of Management Studies, 33*(5), 667–700.

Brandstätter, H. (2011). Personality aspects of entrepreneurship: A look at five meta-analyses. *Personality and Individual Differences, 51*(3), 222–230.

Campbell, W. K., Goodie, A. S., & Foster, J. D. (2004). Narcissism, confidence, and risk attitude. *Journal of Behavioral Decision Making, 17*(4), 297–311.

Cefis, E., & Marsili, O. (2005). A matter of life and death: Innovation and firm survival. *Industrial and Corporate Change, 14*(6), 1167–1192.

Chamorro-Premuzic, T., & Reichenbacher, L. (2008). Effects of personality and threat of evaluation on divergent and convergent thinking. *Journal of Research in Personality, 42*(4), 1095–1101.

Chatterjee, A., & Hambrick, D. C. (2007). It's all about me: Narcissistic chief executive officers and their effects on company strategy and performance. *Administrative Science Quarterly, 52*(3), 351–386.

Ciavarella, M. A., Buchholtz, A. K., Riordan, C. M., Gatewood, R. D., & Stokes, G. S. (2004). The Big Five and venture survival: Is there a linkage? *Journal of Business Venturing, 19*(4), 465–483.

Coad, A., Segarra, A., & Teruel, M. (2016). Innovation and firm growth: Does firm age play a role? *Research Policy, 45*(2), 387–400.

Dahl, D. W., & Moreau, P. (2002). The influence and value of analogical thinking during new product ideation. *Journal of Marketing Research, 39*(1), 47–60.

De Hoogh, A. H., Den Hartog, D. N., & Koopman, P. L. (2005). Linking the Big Five-Factors of personality to charismatic and transactional leadership; perceived dynamic work environment as a moderator. *Journal of Organizational Behavior, 26*(7), 839–865.

de Vries, R. E. (2008). What are we measuring? Convergence of leadership with interpersonal and non-interpersonal personality. *Leadership, 4*(4), 403–417.

Eastman, J. K., Eastman, K. L., & Tolson, M. A. (2001). The relationship between ethical ideology and ethical behavior intentions: An exploratory look at physicians' responses to managed care dilemmas. *Journal of Business Ethics, 31*(3), 209–224.

Freeman, C. (1995). The "National System of Innovation" in historical perspective. *Cambridge Journal of Economics, 19*(1), 5–24.

Furnham, A., & Bachtiar, V. (2008). Personality and intelligence as predictors of creativity. *Personality and Individual Differences, 45*(7), 613–617.

Furnham, A., Batey, M., Anand, K., & Manfield, J. (2008). Personality, hypomania, intelligence and creativity. *Personality and Individual Differences, 44*(5), 1060–1069.

Gal, D. (2019). The genius dilemma: Fortune 1000 CEO personality and firm innovation. *The Journal of Creative Behavior, 53*(3), 339–348.

García-Sánchez, E., García-Morales, V. J., & Martín-Rojas, R. (2018). Analysis of the influence of the environment, stakeholder integration capability, absorptive capacity, and technological skills on organizational performance through corporate entrepreneurship. *International Entrepreneurship and Management Journal, 14*(2), 345–377.

Gelade, G. A. (2002). Creative style, personality, and artistic endeavor. *Genetic, Social, and General Psychology Monographs, 128*(3), 213–234.

Goncalo, J. A., Flynn, F. J., & Kim, S. H. (2010). Are two narcissists better than one? The link between narcissism, perceived creativity, and creative performance. *Personality and Social Psychology Bulletin, 36*(11), 1484–1495.

Groenewegen, G., & de Langen, F. (2012). Critical success factors of the survival of start-ups with a radical innovation. *Journal of Applied Economics & Business Research, 2*(3), 155–171.

Hambrick, D. C., & Mason, P. A. (1984). Upper echelons: The organization as a reflection of its top managers. *Academy of Management Review, 9*(2), 193–206.

Hare, R. D. (1999). *Without conscience: The disturbing world of the psychopaths among us.* New York, NY: Guilford Press.

Hare, R. D., & Neumann, C. S. (2006). The PCL-R assessment of psychopathy. In C. J. Patrick (Ed.), *Handbook of psychopathy* (pp. 58–88). New York, NY: Guilford Press.

Hausman, A. (2005). Innovativeness among small businesses: Theory and propositions for future research. *Industrial Marketing Management, 34*(8), 773–782.

Helmers, C., & Rogers, M. (2011). Does patenting help high-tech start-ups? *Research Policy, 40*(7), 1016–1027.

Hmieleski, K. M., & Lerner, D. A. (2016). The Dark Triad and nascent entrepreneurship: An examination of unproductive versus productive entrepreneurial motives. *Journal of Small Business Management, 54*, 7–32.

Hsieh, H.-L., Hsieh, J.-R., & Wang, I.-L. (2011). Linking personality and innovation: The role of knowledge management. *World Transactions on Engineering and Technology Education, 9*(1), 38–44.

Huber, F. (2012). On the role and interrelationship of spatial, social and cognitive proximity: Personal knowledge relationships of R&D workers in the Cambridge information technology cluster. *Regional Studies, 46*(9), 1169–1182.

Hutter, K., Füller, J., Hautz, J., Bilgram, V., & Matzler, K. (2015). Machiavellianism or morality: Which behavior pays off in online innovation contests? *Journal of Management Information Systems, 32*(3), 197–228.

John, O. P., & Srivastava, S. (1999). The Big Five trait taxonomy: History, measurement, and theoretical perspectives. In L. A. Pervin & O. P. John (Eds.), *Handbook of personality: Theory and research* (2nd ed., pp. 102–138). New York, NY: Guilford Press.

Jonason, P. K., & Krause, L. (2013). The emotional deficits associated with the Dark Triad traits: Cognitive empathy, affective empathy, and alexithymia. *Personality and Individual Differences, 55*(5), 532–537.

Jonason, P. K., Li, N. P., & Teicher, E. A. (2010). Who is James Bond? The Dark Triad as an agentic social style. *Individual Differences Research, 8*(2), 111–120.

Jonason, P. K., & Tost, J. (2010). I just cannot control myself: The Dark Triad and self-control. *Personality and Individual Differences, 49*(6), 611–615.

Jonason, P. K., & Webster, G. D. (2010). The dirty dozen: A concise measure of the Dark Triad. *Psychological Assessment, 22*(2), 420–432.

Jones, D. N. (2013). What's mine is mine and what's yours is mine: The Dark Triad and gambling with your neighbor's money. *Journal of Research in Personality, 47*(5), 563–571.

Jones, D. N., & Figueredo, A. J. (2013). The core of darkness: Uncovering the heart of the Dark Triad. *European Journal of Personality, 27*(6), 521–531.

Judge, T. A., & Bono, J. E. (2000). Five-factor model of personality and transformational leadership. *Journal of Applied Psychology, 85*(5), 751–765.

Julian, C. C., & Terjesen, S. (2006). *Entrepreneurial aspirations – a five country study* [Paper presentation]. 11th Annual Conference of Asia Pacific Decision Sciences Institute, Chinese University of Hong Kong.

Jung, D. I., Chow, C., & Wu, A. (2003). The role of transformational leadership in enhancing organizational innovation: Hypotheses and some preliminary findings. *The Leadership Quarterly, 14*(4–5), 525–544.

Keller, R. T. (2006). Transformational leadership, initiating structure, and substitutes for leadership: A longitudinal study of research and development project team performance. *Journal of Applied Psychology, 91*(1), 202–210.

Kickul, J., & Gundry, L. (2002). Prospecting for strategic advantage: The proactive entrepreneurial personality and small firm innovation. *Journal of Small Business Management, 40*(2), 85–97.

King, N. (2004). Using interviews in quantitative research. In C. Cassel & S. Gillian (Eds.), *Essential guide to qualitative methods in organizational research* (pp. 11–22). London: SAGE.

Kornish, L. J., & Ulrich, K. T. (2014). The importance of the raw idea in innovation: Testing the sow's ear hypothesis. *Journal of Marketing Research, 51*(1), 14–26.

Lefcourt, H. M. (2014). *Locus of control: Current trends in theory & research.* New York, NY: Psychology Press.

Leonelli, S., Ceci, F., & Masciarelli, F. (2016). The importance of entrepreneurs' traits in explaining start-ups' innovativeness. *Sinergie: Italian Journal of Management, 34*(101), 71–85.

Levine, D. S., & Sichelman, T. (2019). Why do startups use trade secrets? *Notre Dame Law Review, 94*(2), 751–820.

Lonial, S. C., & Carter, R. E. (2015). The impact of organizational orientations on medium and small firm performance: A resource-based perspective. *Journal of Small Business Management, 53*(1), 94–113.

Maccoby, M. (2000). Narcissistic leaders: The incredible pros, the inevitable cons. *Harvard Business Review, 78*(1), 68–78.

Maccoby, M. (2003). *The productive narcissist: The promise and peril of visionary leadership.* New York, NY: Broadway Books.

Major, D. A., Turner, J. E., & Fletcher, T. D. (2006). Linking proactive personality and the Big Five to motivation to learn and development activity. *Journal of Applied Psychology, 91*(4), 927–935.

Marcati, A., Guido, G., & Peluso, A. M. (2008). The role of SME entrepreneurs' innovativeness and personality in the adoption of innovations. *Research Policy, 37*(9), 1579–1590.

Martindale, C., & Dailey, A. (1996). Creativity, primary process cognition and personality. *Personality and Individual Differences, 20*(4), 409–414.

McCrae, R. R., & Costa, P. T. (1999). A five-factor theory of personality. In L. A. Pervin and O. P. John (Eds.), *Handbook of personality: Theory and research* (2nd ed., pp. 159–181). New York, NY: Guilford Press.

McKenny, A. F., Aguinis, H., Short, J. C., & Anglin, A. H. (2018). What doesn't get measured does exist: Improving the accuracy of computer-aided text analysis. *Journal of Management, 44*(7), 2909–2933.

Miller, D., Kets de Vries, M. F., & Toulouse, J.-M. (1982). Top executive locus of control and its relationship to strategy-making, structure, and environment. *Academy of Management Journal, 25*(2), 237–253.

Miller, D., & Toulouse, J.-M. (1986). Chief executive personality and corporate strategy and structure in small firms. *Management Science, 32*(11), 1389–1409.

Papadakis, V., & Bourantas, D. (1998). The chief executive officer as corporate champion of technological innovation: An empirical investigation. *Technology Analysis & Strategic Management, 10*(1), 89–110.

Parker, S. C. (2004). *The economics of self-employment and entrepreneurship.* Cambridge, UK: Cambridge University Press.

Patterson, F. (2002). Great minds don't think alike? Person-level predictors of innovation at work. *International Review of Industrial and Organizational Psychology, 17*, 115–144.

Paulsen, N., Maldonado, D., Callan, V. J., & Ayoko, O. (2009). Charismatic leadership, change and innovation in an R&D organization. *Journal of Organizational Change Management, 22*(5), 511–523.

Rauch, A., & Frese, M. (2007). Let's put the person back into entrepreneurship research: A meta-analysis on the relationship between business owners' personality traits, business creation, and success. *European Journal of Work and Organizational Psychology, 16*(4), 353–385.

Rodríguez-Pose, A., & Storper, M. (2006). Better rules or stronger communities? On the social foundations of institutional change and its economic effects. *Economic Geography, 82*(1), 1–25.

Rothmann, S., & Coetzer, E. P. (2003). The Big Five personality dimensions and job performance. *SA Journal of Industrial Psychology, 29*(1), 68–74.

Rotter, J. B. (1954). *Social learning and clinical psychology.* New York, NY: Prentice Hall.

Rotter, J. B. (1966). Generalized expectancies for internal versus external control of reinforcement. *Psychological monographs: General and applied, 80*(1), 1–28.

Rouhizadeh, M., Jaidka, K., Smith, L., Schwartz, H. A., Buffone, A., & Ungar, L. (2018). *Identifying locus of control in social media language* [Paper presentation]. 2018 Conference on Empirical Methods in Natural Language Processing, Brussels, Belgium.

Sakalaki, M., Richardson, C., & Thépaut, Y. (2007). Machiavellianism and economic opportunism. *Journal of Applied Social Psychology, 37*(6), 1181–1190.

Samuelsson, M., & Davidsson, P. (2009). Does venture opportunity variation matter? Investigating systematic process differences between innovative and imitative new ventures. *Small Business Economics, 33*(2), 229–255.

Smith, M. B., & Webster, B. D. (2018). Narcissus the innovator? The relationship between grandiose narcissism, innovation, and adaptability. *Personality and Individual Differences, 121,* 67–73.

Song, M., Podoynitsyna, K., Van der Bij, H., & Halman, J. I. (2008). Success factors in new ventures: A meta-analysis. *Journal of Product Innovation Management, 25*(1), 7–27.

Sosik, J. J., Kahai, S. S., & Avolio, B. J. (1998). Transformational leadership and dimensions of creativity: Motivating idea generation in computer-mediated groups. *Creativity Research Journal, 11*(2), 111–121.

Sumner, C., Byers, A., Boochever, R., & Park, G. J. (2012). *Predicting Dark Triad personality traits from Twitter usage and a linguistic analysis of tweets* [Paper presentation]. 11th International Conference on Machine Learning and Applications (ICMLA), Boca Raton, Florida, USA.

Vecchio, R. P. (2003). Entrepreneurship and leadership: Common trends and common threads. *Human Resource Management Review, 13*(2), 303–327.

Woo, S. E., Chernyshenko, O. S., Longley, A., Zhang, Z.-X., Chiu, C.-Y., & Stark, S. E. (2014). Openness to experience: Its lower level structure, measurement, and cross-cultural equivalence. *Journal of Personality Assessment, 96*(1), 29–45.

Yarkoni, T. (2010). Personality in 100,000 words: A large-scale analysis of personality and word use among bloggers. *Journal of Research in Personality, 44*(3), 363–373.

Zahra, S. A. (1996). Governance, ownership, and corporate entrepreneurship: The moderating impact of industry technological opportunities. *Academy of Management Journal, 39*(6), 1713–1735.

Zhao, H., & Seibert, S. E. (2006). The Big Five personality dimensions and entrepreneurial status: A meta-analytical review. *Journal of Applied Psychology, 91*(2), 259–271.

Zhao, H., Seibert, S. E., & Lumpkin, G. T. (2010). The relationship of personality to entrepreneurial intentions and performance: A meta-analytic review. *Journal of Management, 36*(2), 381–404.

Zhao, L., & Jung, H.-B. (2018). The winning personality: Impact of founders' personality traits and firms' network relationships on Chinese apparel new venture performance. *International Journal of Entrepreneurial Behavior & Research, 24*(2), 553–573.

Zibarras, L. D., Port, R. L., & Woods, S. A. (2008). Innovation and the "dark side" of personality: Dysfunctional traits and their relation to self-reported innovative characteristics. *The Journal of Creative Behavior, 42*(3), 201–215.

Table A4.1   LIWC dimensions and personality traits

LIWC Dimension	Label	Examples	Big Five					Locus of Control		Dark Traits		
			Openness	Conscient-iousness	Extra-version	Agree-ableness	Neuroticism	Internal	External	Narcissism	Machiavell-ianism	Psycho-pathy
Language metrics												
Words > 6 letters	Sixltr	Words > 6 letters									−	
Dictionary words	Dic	Dictionary words								−		
Total pronouns	pronoun	I, them, itself	− −									
1st pers. singular	i	I, me, mine	− −						+ +			
1st pers plural	we	We, us, our				+ +		− −			−	−
2nd pers.	you	You			+ +		− −					
3rd pers singular	shehe	he/she, him/her						− −				
Articles	article	the, a, an	+ +									
Prepositions	prep	To, with, above	+ +					+ +	+ +			−
Auxiliary verbs	auxverb	Am, will, have						+ +	+ +			

LIWC Dimension	Label	Examples	Big Five					Locus of Control		Dark Traits		
			Openness	Conscientiousness	Extraversion	Agreeableness	Neuroticism	Internal	External	Narcissism	Machiavellianism	Psychopathy
Negations	negate	No, not, never		– –							+	
Interrogatives	interrog							+ +				
Numbers	number	Second, thousand									+	
Quantifiers	quant	Few, many, much								–		
Affect words	affect	Happy, cried, abandon										
Positive emotion	posemo	Love, nice, sweet	– –			+ +		– –				–
Negative emotion	negemo	Hurt, ugly, nasty		– –		– –	+ +		– –			+
Anxiety	anx	Worried, fearful					+ +		– –	–		
Anger	anger	Hate, kill, annoyed		– –		– –						+
Sadness	sad	Crying, grief, sad							+ +			
Social words	social	Mate, talk, they, child			+ +				+ +		–	
Family	family	Daughter, husband,	– –			+ +						
Friends	friend	Buddy, friend			+ +					+		
Cognitive processes	cogproc	cause, know, ought							+ +	–		
Discrepancies	discrep	should, would, could							+ +			

			Big Five					Locus of Control		Dark Traits		
LIWC Dimension	Label	Examples	Openness	Conscientiousness	Extraversion	Agreeableness	Neuroticism	Internal	External	Narcissism	Machiavellianism	Psychopathy
Negations	negate	No, not, never		- -							+	
Interrogatives	interrog							+ +				
Numbers	number	Second, thousand									+	
Quantifiers	quant	Few, many, much								-		
Affect words	affect	Happy, cried, abandon									-	
Positive emotion	posemo	Love, nice, sweet	- -			+ +		- -				-
Negative emotion	negemo	Hurt, ugly, nasty		- -		- -	+ +		- -			+
Anxiety	anx	Worried, fearful					+ +		- -			
Anger	anger	Hate, kill, annoyed		- -		- -						+
Sadness	sad	Crying, grief, sad							+ +			
Social words	social	Mate, talk, they, child	- -		+ +							
Family	family	Daughter, husband,				+ +					-	
Friends	friend	Buddy, friend	- -		+ +					+		
Cognitive processes	cogproc	cause, know, ought							+ +	-		
Discrepancies	discrep	should, would, could							+ +			

LIWC Dimension	Label	Examples	Big Five					Locus of Control		Dark Traits		
			Openness	Conscientiousness	Extraversion	Agreeableness	Neuroticism	Internal	External	Narcissism	Machiavellianism	Psychopathy
Religion	relig		+ +					+ +				
Death	death	Bury, coffin, kill										+
Swear words	swear	Damn, piss, fuck				– –					+	+
Fillers	filler	Blah, Imean, youknow									+	+
All punctuation												
Dashes	Dash	–									–	
Quotation marks	Quote	""								+		
Apostrophes	Apostro									–		
Other punctuation	OtherP	#@								+		

Note: + + statistically significant positive correlation ($p < 0.01$); – – statistically significant negative correlation ($p < 0.01$); + statistically significant positive correlation ($p < 0.05$), – statistically significant negative correlation ($p < 0.05$).

5. Entrepreneurial personality and small business financing

5.1 INTRODUCTION

Start-up companies are newly founded companies or entrepreneurial ventures that are in a phase of development and market research (Klačmer Čalopa, Horvat, & Lalić, 2014). Their primary business concern relies on the financing process, mainly because investors are looking for a combination of the highest potential return on investments and the lowest associated risks (Van Osnabrugge, 2000).

In the light of the above framework, one of the most significant challenges entrepreneurs face is to present their ventures in a favorable light and to arouse a compelling interest in investors to fund their business idea (Cornelissen & Clarke, 2010; Lounsbury & Glynn, 2001; Mayhew & Pike, 2004). On the other side, investors have very little information and their impressions might be more or less based on subjective judgments (Maxwell, Jeffrey, & Lévesque, 2011); in fact, investors might invest before more reliable reputation-related information comes into existence (Elsbach & Kramer, 2003; Parhankangas & Ehrlich, 2014).

Business angel networks and other private investor agencies sometimes invite entrepreneurs to pitch their idea or to describe their newborn ventures, organizing events such as investor forums or enterprise dinner clubs (Mason & Harrison, 2003; Payne & Macarty, 2002). Entrepreneurs need to take full advantage of these interesting opportunities. Through their pitch they can present their idea and try to attract and persuade investors. The main objectives are arousing investors' curiosity and trying to obtain an appointment to discuss the investment opportunity in detail. If entrepreneurs are unable to convince and attract anyone, they are likely to seriously compromise their chances of receiving funds (Clark, 2008). However, receiving funding is always beneficial even when entrepreneurs have only a business idea or if the firm has just been founded, because attracting investors is an excellent opportunity for creating or growing a business (Bonnet & Wirtz, 2012).

We focus principally on two types of investors such as business angels (BAs) and venture capitalists (VCs). BAs are active investors who enjoy the process of helping a company and actively providing advice and connections, thus enabling its growth and survival (Harrison & Mason, 2000). By providing external capital and offering valuable guidance and coaching, BAs serve as a signal to larger investors that the venture is worth consideration (Kaiser, Lauterbach, & Verweyen, 2007; Murnieks, Sudek, & Wiltbank, 2015). VCs raise funds from individuals, organizations, pension funds, governments, insurance companies, and so on, and invest them in early-stage ventures that offer high reward potential through an equity stake, yet also a high risk (Wallmeroth, Wirtz, & Groh, 2018). The main differences between BAs and VCs are in the way they find, approach, finance, and actually help the firm. First, BAs and VCs play a complementary role in terms of financing different stages of business development; in particular, BAs invest in the very early stage of the start-up, while VCs arrive at a later stage when the start-up is more solid (Harrison & Mason, 2000). Second, VCs use sophisticated "due diligence" and term-sheet tools to build a solid investment portfolio (Cumming, Schmidt, & Walz, 2010), while BAs have less formal procedures and use personal relationships to select their projects and decide to invest (Ding, Sun, & Au, 2014; Sudek, 2006).

This chapter aims to illustrate how entrepreneurs' way of presenting themselves (i.e., through their personality traits) and their behavior affect their likelihood of securing funding and the amount of funding itself. We add new insights to the growing body of research showing that entrepreneurs' communication skills and personal attributes influence investor decision-making.

The remainder of this chapter is structured as follows. We begin by exploring the main types of business financing sources and discussing the extant literature on the importance of personality traits in attracting small business funding. Then, we formulate two hypotheses on how entrepreneurs' narcissism affects the likelihood of receiving funding. Finally, we propose a description of the research method, an analysis of the results, as well as a discussion and conclusion.

5.2 ANALYSIS OF SMALL BUSINESS FINANCING SOURCES

Collecting funds for start-ups is not as easy as it is for already established companies (Di Pietro, Prencipe, & Majchrzak, 2018). Investors who want to know the real value of an investment should consider the present value of future cash flows. However, it is hard to apply this calculation to start-ups because they do not have a previous profit history or account-ing information (Barth, Cram, & Nelson, 2001). Despite this, there are different opportunities for start-ups to collect funds and these depend upon their stage of development (i.e., idea, prototype, or launch) and the respective amount of money they need. Figure 5.1 depicts the common start-up's phases and the related type of funding and profit.

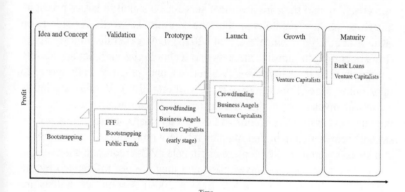

Figure 5.1   Start-up phases and financing

Bootstrapping means entrepreneur self-funding from the ground up and building the company up with cash coming in from first sales. The use of one's own money implies that the entrepreneur has a good income and that the creation of the start-up does not require a large amount of funds (Ebben & Johnson, 2006). Friends, family and fools (FFF, 3Fs) are a financing source for entrepreneurs before applying for external sources of funding. Entrepreneurs try to convince relatives and close friends to invest in their business idea. The answer of the 3Fs to this call for funds is a signal for future investors because it shows that the entrepreneur believes in his or her own project and his or her close friends are willing to take part in this risk (Kotha & George, 2012).

Bank loans are the other side of the coin and they allow entrepreneurs who do not have money of their own to obtain some funds and start their business. However, start-up entrepreneurs find very difficult to receive bank loans because of the long and complex bureaucratic process requiring abundant information on individual credit history and properties (Åstebro & Bernhardt, 2003). Public funds provide financial support by the public at a local, national, or EU level. Start-ups can benefit from these funds by producing products or services that are of public interest (i.e., with a public value potential) (Colombo, Grilli, & Verga, 2007).

Business angels are themselves entrepreneurs or experts in the field that decided to share their know-how, experience, and financial resources with the new venture's entrepreneur. BAs provide valuable guidance and coaching and their involvement serves as a signal to larger investors (such as venture capitalists) that the venture is worth consideration (Kaiser et al., 2007; Murnieks et al., 2015). BAs generally invest only in firms operating in familiar markets and technologies and that are closely congruent with their investment objectives, and geographically closer to their home base (Prasad, Vozikis, & Bruton, 2001). Venture capital is a form of investment with different origins; it can be provided by individuals, corporations, or funds. As opposed to bank loans, which for the start-up represent a debt that must be repaid within a specific time period at a specific interest rate, venture capitalists (VCs) require a share of the equity in return for their investment and they are not influenced by the start-up's cash flow (Gompers & Lerner, 2000). Venture capitalists are the embodiment of formal investors: they supply specialized and formal funds, supporting the expansion stages that precede the flow into capital markets, and they play a determining role in the management of start-ups, sitting on the boards of directors (Prasad et al., 2001). Table 5.1 summarizes similarities and differences between BAs and VCs.

Crowdfunding is the newest way for start-ups to receive funds. Through the use of the Internet, start-ups have the possibility to find capital contributors, to have a floor for marketing, and to determine the demand, while investors can be rewarded for their grants through attractive offers on products or acknowledgments (Wallmeroth et al., 2018). These consist in collective fund-raising via social networks and ICTs (Di Pietro, 2019).

Table 5.1   Differences between BAs and VCs

Key Features	Business Angels	Institutional Venture Capitalists
Type of funds	Money of private individuals	People's money invested by institutional investors
Responsibility	Significant personal financial responsibility	Limited personal financial responsibility but responsibility to management and owners
Time for due diligence	Limited time	Extensive time
Investment stage	Early stage	Early and later stage
Operational engagement	Some hours per week	Some hours per month
Exit strategy	Less important	Very important
Length of holding period	Three to eight years	Three to five years

Source: Our elaboration based on Avdeitchikova, Landström, and Månsson (2008).

5.3   SMALL BUSINESS FINANCING (VENTURE CAPITALISTS AND BUSINESS ANGELS) AND PERSONALITY TRAITS

Previous studies on small business financing provide a long list of variables that could affect investors' decisions. Among these are the characteristics of the product/service, the target market, the entrepreneur, the firm, and the predicted financial performance (see Mason & Harrison, 2003; Mason & Stark, 2004; Maxwell et al., 2011; Sudek, 2006; Zacharakis & Meyer, 1998). However, sometimes it is impossible to focus on a new firm's products or services or on its characteristics because of the lack of information and data at the time of investors' decision (Parhankangas & Ehrlich, 2014). Thus, considering the impressions created by entrepreneurs is the only way to get an idea of the quality of the investment and, in this case, the entrepreneur's personality matters.

Previous studies investigate the existence of a link between personality and entrepreneurial outcomes (Ciavarella, Buchholtz, Riordan, Gatewood, & Stokes, 2004; Murnieks et al., 2015; Zhao & Seibert, 2006; Zhao, Seibert, & Lumpkin, 2010). However, few studies analyze how personality traits impact on small business financing. In particular, the majority of them investigate how relatively tangible and verifiable "human capital" factors such as skills, experience, entrepreneurs' visible characteristics (i.e., age, levels of education, and gender) can be important for investors to decide whether they should finance a firm or not (Haines, Madill, & Riding, 2003; Mason & Stark, 2004; Sudek, 2006; Van Osnabrugge, 2000). Only a small number of these works consider other more subjective, far less tangible "human" factors such as the personal attributes, social competencies and communication skills of the entrepreneurs and how these influence investors' decisions (Ding et al., 2014).

Regarding the attraction of VCs: MacMillan, Siegel, and Narasimha (1985) identified the main entrepreneurs' characteristics that are essential to convincing VCs to invest in their ideas. These are (1) readiness, proactiveness, and motivation, which enable entrepreneurs to sustain intense effort; (2) risk-proneness and risk-taking that allow entrepreneurs to evaluate and react well to risks; (3) finally, being showmen and women enables them to persuade peers and employees (but also investors) and incentivizes discussion within the firm. Fried and Hisrich (1994), on the other hand, show that personal integrity, realism, and flexibility are the favorable characteristics that entrepreneurs should possess to receive VCs' funding.

Regarding the attraction of BAs, Feeney, Haines Jr., and Riding (1999) show that openness to experience, honesty, realism, and integrity are important characteristics that entrepreneurs should possess to attract BAs' investments. Haines et al. (2003) add the aspects of ethicality and foresight to the above features. Murnieks et al. (2015) confirm that BAs consider the entrepreneur personality when evaluating start-ups for investment opportunities and identify some important characteristics. They show that conscientiousness and low levels of agreeableness are fundamental because they lead to hard work, meticulousness, and relentlessness in building the venture. Moreover, extraversion and emotional stability are beneficial as well. Finally, when analyzing the impact of the entrepreneur's pitch on BAs, Clark (2008) shows that authenticity and passion draw BAs' attention, while apathy and arrogance are detrimental.

In general, VCs and BAs prefer to be affiliated with happy individuals, since happiness contributes to perceived intelligence and competencies (Lyubomirsky, King, & Diener, 2005; Murnieks et al., 2015; Van Kleef, De Dreu, & Manstead, 2010).

5.4 ENTREPRENEURIAL NARCISSISM AND THE IMPACT ON BUSINESS ANGEL AND VENTURE CAPITAL INVESTMENTS

The term narcissism encompasses an individual's set of attitudes, acts, and considerations in the management of self-esteem. Generally, it includes a set of egocentric traits such as self-admiration, self-centeredness, and self-regard (Goncalo, Flynn, & Kim, 2010; Sedikides, Rudich, Gregg, Kumashiro, & Rusbult, 2004). Highly narcissistic individuals have a strong sense of entitlement and a constant need for attention and admiration (Bogart, Benotsch, & Pavlovic, 2004); they tend to emerge as leaders (Brunell et al., 2008), even at the highest levels of organizations (Chatterjee & Hambrick, 2007).

Empowering and investing in the relationship between BAs or VCs and entrepreneurs proves essential because of the existence of an information asymmetry between the parties (Aernoudt, 2005; Davila, Foster, & Gupta, 2003). Trust can help to reduce these asymmetries, allowing them to build a strong and lasting relationship (Kollmann, Kuckertz, & Middelberg, 2014). Thus, a process of trust-building is needed, both before and after the investment – before the investment because trust in entrepreneurs influences investors' selection criteria, and after the investment because entrepreneurs and investors work side by side for the start-up's growth and survival (Harrison, Dibben, & Mason, 1997). However, this is only possible if the entrepreneurs' personality traits match and satisfy the investors' requirements.

We posit that narcissistic entrepreneurs are more able to attract BAs' and VCs' investments than their non-narcissistic counterparts. We identify two mechanisms through which narcissism works: the persuasive effect and the commitment effect. The persuasive effect helps narcissists to gain support and reassurance from investors and followers. In general, narcissists employ the art of rhetoric to persuade, influence, and mobilize others (Maccoby, 2000). The expressions they use are spontaneous and encouraging, especially if they know that they are being listened to and admired by others (Maccoby, 2003). The likability and attractiveness of narcissistic entrepreneurs who pitch ideas to investors enables them to receive support even if their ideas are unexceptional (Goncalo et al., 2010; Parhankangas & Ehrlich, 2014). In fact, a positive first impression on investors increases the perceived credibility of the person being observed and facilitates collaboration; this phenomenon is called opinion conformity (Byrne, 1971; O'Keefe, 2002; Perloff, 2008). Moreover, the use of positive language can improve the success of the persuasive effect. Narcissistic entrepreneurs succeed in convincing and reassuring investors through their way of expressing themselves and putting their business idea forward (Elsbach & Kramer, 2003; Grijalva & Harms, 2014) through a clever use of positive language. By using positive statements or even boasting about their organizations, they may signal competence, confidence, and ambition (Parhankangas & Ehrlich, 2014; Short & Palmer, 2008) and this increases the likelihood of receiving more capital.

The commitment effect shows how narcissists work hard to reach their goals (Miller, 2015; Paulhus & Williams, 2002). Their augmented self-view leads narcissistic entrepreneurs to be overoptimistic and over-confident about their abilities and their start-ups' positive results, which will result from the way narcissistic entrepreneurs engage in projects that their non-narcissistic counterparts consider infeasible or too risky. Narcissistic entrepreneurs generally develop a strong and compelling vision for their firms, making sure that they do everything they can to achieve the objectives set. According to Prasad et al. (2001), a signal of entrepreneur commitment is fundamental for BAs and VCs. Start-ups typically face turbulent environments in which business failure can occur quickly; thus, the absence of commitment effect may indicate an absence of appropriate control and monitoring by the entrepreneur. BAs and VCs may then perceive a greater chance of financial loss (Prasad et al., 2001). On the other hand, the commitment effect of narcissistic entrepreneurs may help BAs and VCs to evaluate more accurately which new endeavors are worth funding.

These arguments suggest a positive effect of entrepreneur narcissism on BAs and VCs investments in start-ups. Thus, we put forward the following hypotheses:

Hypothesis 1 (H_1): Entrepreneur narcissism positively influences the number of business angels who invest in the business.

Hypothesis 2 (H_2): Entrepreneur narcissism positively influences the number of venture capitalists who invest in the business.

5.5 EMPIRICAL STRATEGY

5.5.1 Sample and Procedure

The study focuses on Chinese start-ups, and the reason for our choice is related to the generally accepted idea that Chinese people, indeed, most Asians, for historical and cultural reasons, tend to be less selfish and narcissistic than Europeans and Americans.

We had great difficulty in getting access to official registers of Chinese start-ups. Furthermore, we encountered problems in finding financial information on databases, mainly because the Chinese government tends not to disclose data. Thus, to select our sample, we looked for unofficial reliable sources, such as the website angel.co. This website contains information on 3 055 782 worldwide start-ups and 5658 Chinese start-ups in particular. Information includes a description of the start-up activity, the head office location, the number of employees, the industry it works in, the year of foundation, the names of founders, major employees and advisors, and the investors, including venture capitalists and business angels.

We randomly selected 250 companies and we contacted entrepreneurs in different ways depending on whether they were registered on LinkedIn. For those who did not have a LinkedIn profile, we contacted them via Twitter, WeChat, or via their personal email address. For each type of social network, the procedure was always the same. We used our personal profiles to introduce ourselves and the study: 197 entrepreneurs (79 percent) responded to our invitation. We sent these 197 entrepreneurs a link to an electronic survey to assess their level of narcissism. To increase response rates, we told entrepreneurs that, at the end of the study, they would receive a personalized report about the study. We received 70 responses, but five of them were incomplete, therefore we were able to use only 65 questionnaires (response rate of 26 percent). The survey was both in English and in Chinese and it was administered between March and June 2017. The questionnaire comprised two sections: the first included 16 questions to measure entrepreneurs' narcissism (Ames, Rose, & Anderson, 2006); the second asked for personal details such as entrepreneur's name, age, sex, and number of owned firms.

Table 5.2 lists the main characteristics of the small businesses and entrepreneurs sampled. In particular, small firms mainly belong to the communication and information industry, they are predominantly located

Table 5.2   *Characteristics of firms and entrepreneurs*

Small Firm Characteristics	N	%	Entrepreneur Characteristics	N	%
Industry			*Education*		
Commerce	65	4.6	High school	65	6.2
Communication and information		27.7	Bachelor's degree		41.5
Education		9.2	Master's degree		41.5
Financial		7.7	PhD		10.8
Food and beverage		6.1			
Health		7.9			
Manufacturing		13.9			
Recruiting		3.0			
Software		12.3			
Transportation		4.6			
Travel		3.0			
Location			Age		
Beijing	65	26.2	< 30 years old	65	26.2
Guangzhou		1.5	30–39 years old		44.6
Haikou		1.5	40–49 years old		15.4
Hangzhou		3.1	> 50 years old		13.8
Shanghai		44.6			
Shenzhen		23.1			
Employees			Gender		
1–10	62*	61.3	Male	65	89.2
11–50		25.8	Female		10.8
> 50		12.9			

Note: *Data not available for the whole sample.

in Shanghai, and they are very small, with between one and ten employees. The entrepreneurs are mainly educated to bachelor's and master's degree levels of education, they are aged between 30 and 39, and they are principally male.

5.5.2   Measures

In Study 1 we considered two dependent variables: the number of business angels (i.e., #BA) and the number of venture capitalists (i.e., #VC) who invested in the start-up. These variables are both continuous and represent the real number of business angels and venture capitalists who respectively invest in the start-up.

Table 5.3   Descriptive statistics

Variable	Mean	SD	Min	Max
#BA	1.062	2.169	0	14
#VC	0.692	0.991	0	3
Entrepreneur narcissism				
Narcissism_3	3.785	1.154	1	5
Narcissism_4	3.354	1.302	1	5
Narcissism_13	3.723	1.103	1	5
Narcissism_15	3.615	1.077	1	5
Narcissism_16	3.538	0.068	1	5

Note: $N = 65$.

The independent variable is *entrepreneur narcissism* and the Narcissistic Personality Inventory 16-item (NPI-16) survey designed by Ames et al. (2006) was used to measure it. We adopted a five-point Likert scale version developed by Gentile (2013), removing the non-narcissistic statement from each item. The NPI-16 original version is in English and to ensure an accurate translation into Chinese, a rigorous back-translation technique was employed (Brislin, 1980). A bilingual English-Chinese speaker translated the questionnaire from English into Chinese, and then another bilingual speaker translated the Chinese version back into English. These two linguistic versions of the questionnaires were both sent to the entrepreneurs; in this way, they could choose which one they preferred to answer.

5.5.3   Results

Table 5.3 shows the descriptive statistics of our sample. The research model was analyzed using Smart PLS, a partial least squares (PLS) structural equation modeling tool. Following the recommendations of Hulland (1999), the PLS model was analyzed in two stages: first testing the measurement model adequacy and then assessing the structural model. The first stage included the estimation of individual item reliability (Cronbach's alpha > 0.70), the composite reliabilities (CRs > 0.70), and the average amount of variance (AVE > 0.50). Table 5.4 shows the totality of values.

Table 5.5 presents the results of the testing for the discriminant validity of the measurement scales employed. The elements in the matrix diago-

Table 5.4   *Assessment of the measurement model*

Variable Constructs	Cronbach's Alpha	CR	AVE
Entrepreneur narcissism	0.839	0.881	0.598

Table 5.5   *Discriminant validity (intercorrelation) of variable constructs*

Latent Variables	1	2	3
1. Entrepreneur narcissism	0.773		
2. #BA	0.154	1	
3. #VC	0.254	0.342	1

nals, representing the square roots of the AVEs, are in all cases greater than the off-diagonal elements in their corresponding row and column, supporting the discriminant validity of our variables.

We tested convergent validity by extracting the factor and cross-loadings of all indicator items to their respective latent constructs. These results, presented in Table 5.6, indicated that all items loaded on their respective construct from a lower bound of 0.69 to an upper bound of 0.87; and they loaded more highly on their respective construct than on any other.

Table 5.6   *Factor loadings and cross-loadings*

	#BA	#VC	Entrepreneur Narcissism
#BA	*1.000*	0.342	0.154
#VC	0.342	*1.000*	0.254
Narcissism_3	−0.054	0.076	*0.747*
Narcissism_4	0.114	0.159	*0.694*
Narcissism_13	0.010	0.204	*0.805*
Narcissism_15	0.177	0.192	*0.744*
Narcissism_16	0.166	0.244	*0.865*

Note: Factor loadings are shown in italic.

PLS path analysis allows us to evaluate and test statistical models, using the bootstrapping method (Hayes, 2009). In the present analyses, 5000 bootstrap samples with replacement were requested (Hair, Ringle, & Sarstedt, 2011). Figure 5.2 shows the structural model results. With regard to the relationship between entrepreneur narcissism and the number of business angels who invest in the entrepreneurial idea, results show a positive but not significant relationship (β = 0.154, t = 1.051, p > 0.1), leading us to reject Hypothesis 1. On the other hand, with regard to the relationship between entrepreneur narcissism and the number of venture capitals who invest in the entrepreneurial idea, results show a positive and significant relationship (β = 0.254, t = 2.288, p < 0.05), allowing us to confirm Hypothesis 2.

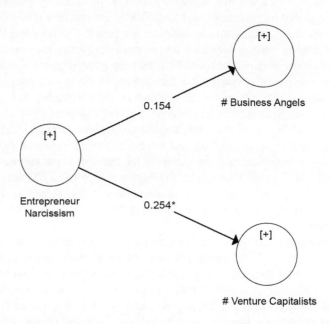

Note: *p <0.05.

Figure 5.2   *The relationship between entrepreneur narcissism and small business financing*

5.6   DISCUSSION AND CONCLUSION

This chapter examined the positive relationship between entrepreneur narcissism and the number of business angels and venture capitalists who invest in the entrepreneurial idea. This result is in line with previous studies considering the importance of entrepreneurs' competence and personality rather than the mere quality of the business idea in BAs' and VCs' decision to invest in start-ups (Mason & Harrison, 2003; Mason & Stark, 2004; Parhankangas & Ehrlich, 2014; Sudek, 2006).

This study makes several theoretical and practical contributions that are important to advancing research in the fields of early start-up investment and entrepreneurship. In the first place, we extend the understanding of the factors that influence investors' decisions by exploring the role played by personality and, specifically, entrepreneur narcissism. Although many studies have investigated the factors that BAs and VCs consider when making decisions, few of them have taken the next step to explore the empirical relationships between entrepreneur narcissism and the number of BAs and VCs they attract. In the second place, we contribute to the entrepreneurship literature by considering how the entrepreneurs' traits and the impressions they create serve as a fundamental role in raising funds. Attracting and impressing investors is critical for new ventures to secure funding, and therefore the entrepreneurial figure plays a very important role since he or she has the tools to put impression strategies into action. Our results highlight the importance of entrepreneurs' expressiveness and persuasiveness to the success of a new venture (Baron & Markman, 2003; Baum, Locke, & Smith, 2001; Parhankangas & Ehrlich, 2014).

From a practical point of view, we provide entrepreneurs with insights into BAs' and VCs' selection policies. As stated many times in this chapter, even if there are a large number of potential investors and large amounts of money, the ability of start-ups to attract funding is extremely limited (Ding et al., 2014). Thus, understanding the investment decision process might help identify the critical reason why an opportunity is rejected as well as increasing the investment success rate.

REFERENCES

Aernoudt, R. (2005). Executive forum: Seven ways to stimulate business angels' investments. *Venture Capital, 7*(4), 359–371.

Ames, D. R., Rose, P., & Anderson, C. P. (2006). The NPI-16 as a short measure of narcissism. *Journal of Research in Personality, 40*(4), 440–450.

Åstebro, T., & Bernhardt, I. (2003). Start-up financing, owner characteristics, and survival. *Journal of Economics and Business, 55*(4), 303–319.

Avdeitchikova, S., Landström, H., & Månsson, N. (2008). What do we mean when we talk about business angels? Some reflections on definitions and sampling. *Venture Capital, 10*(4), 371–394.

Baron, R. A., & Markman, G. D. (2003). Beyond social capital: The role of entrepreneurs' social competence in their financial success. *Journal of Business Venturing, 18*(1), 41–60.

Barth, M. E., Cram, D. P., & Nelson, K. K. (2001). Accruals and the prediction of future cash flows. *The Accounting Review, 76*(1), 27–58.

Baum, J. R., Locke, E. A., & Smith, K. G. (2001). A multidimensional model of venture growth. *Academy of Management Journal, 44*(2), 292–303.

Bogart, L. M., Benotsch, E. G., & Pavlovic, J. D. P. (2004). Feeling superior but threatened: The relation of narcissism to social comparison. *Basic and Applied Social Psychology, 26*(1), 35–44.

Bonnet, C., & Wirtz, P. (2012). Raising capital for rapid growth in young technology ventures: When business angels and venture capitalists coinvest. *Venture Capital, 14*(2–3), 91–110.

Brislin, R. W. (1980). Translation and content analysis of oral and written material. In H. C. Triandis & J. W. Berry (Eds.), *Handbook of cross-cultural psychology: Methodology* (pp. 349–444). Boston, MA: Allyn & Bacon.

Brunell, A. B., Gentry, W. A., Campbell, W. K., Hoffman, B. J., Kuhnert, K. W., & DeMarree, K. G. (2008). Leader emergence: The case of the narcissistic leader. *Personality and Social Psychology Bulletin, 34*(12), 1663–1676.

Byrne, D. E. (1971). *The attraction paradigm.* New York, NY: Academic Press.

Chatterjee, A., & Hambrick, D. C. (2007). It's all about me: Narcissistic chief executive officers and their effects on company strategy and performance. *Administrative Science Quarterly, 52*(3), 351–386.

Ciavarella, M. A., Buchholtz, A. K., Riordan, C. M., Gatewood, R. D., & Stokes, G. S. (2004). The Big Five and venture survival: Is there a linkage? *Journal of Business Venturing, 19*(4), 465–483.

Clark, C. (2008). The impact of entrepreneurs' oral "pitch" presentation skills on business angels' initial screening investment decisions. *Venture Capital, 10*(3), 257–279.

Colombo, M. G., Grilli, L., & Verga, C. (2007). High-tech start-up access to public funds and venture capital: Evidence from Italy. *International Review of Applied Economics, 21*(3), 381–402.

Cornelissen, J. P., & Clarke, J. S. (2010). Imagining and rationalizing opportunities: Inductive reasoning and the creation and justification of new ventures. *Academy of Management Review, 35*(4), 539–557.

Cumming, D., Schmidt, D., & Walz, U. (2010). Legality and venture capital governance around the world. *Journal of Business Venturing, 25*(1), 54–72.

Davila, A., Foster, G., & Gupta, M. (2003). Venture capital financing and the growth of startup firms. *Journal of Business Venturing, 18*(6), 689–708.

Di Pietro, F. (2019). Deciphering crowdfunding. In T. Lynn, J. G. Mooney, P. Rosati, & M. Cummins (Eds.), *Disrupting finance: FinTech and strategy in the 21st century* (pp. 1–14). Cham, Switzerland: Springer International Publishing.

Di Pietro, F., Prencipe, A., & Majchrzak, A. (2018). Crowd equity investors: An underutilized asset for open innovation in startups. *California Management Review, 60*(2), 43–70.

Ding, Z., Sun, S. L., & Au, K. (2014). Angel investors' selection criteria: A comparative institutional perspective. *Asia Pacific Journal of Management, 31*(3), 705–731.

Ebben, J., & Johnson, A. (2006). Bootstrapping in small firms: An empirical analysis of change over time. *Journal of Business Venturing, 21*(6), 851–865.

Elsbach, K. D., & Kramer, R. M. (2003). Assessing creativity in Hollywood pitch meetings: Evidence for a dual-process model of creativity judgments. *The Academy of Management Journal, 46*(3), 283–301.

Feeney, L., Haines Jr., G. H., & Riding, A. L. (1999). Private investors' investment criteria: Insights from qualitative data. *Venture Capital: An International Journal of Entrepreneurial Finance, 1*(2), 121–145.

Fried, V. H., & Hisrich, R. D. (1994). Toward a model of venture capital investment decision making. *Financial Management, 23*(3), 28–37.

Gentile, B. (2013). *Investigating alternative response sets with the Narcissistic Personality Inventory: Validation of a new Likert version* [Doctoral dissertation, University of Georgia].

Gompers, P., & Lerner, J. (2000). Money chasing deals? The impact of fund inflows on private equity valuation. *Journal of Financial Economics, 55*(2), 281–325.

Goncalo, J. A., Flynn, F. J., & Kim, S. H. (2010). Are two narcissists better than one? The link between narcissism, perceived creativity, and creative performance. *Personality and Social Psychology Bulletin, 36*(11), 1484–1495.

Grijalva, E., & Harms, P. D. (2014). Narcissism: An integrative synthesis and dominance complementarity model. *The Academy of Management Perspectives, 28*(2), 108–127.

Haines, G. H. J., Madill, J. J., & Riding, A. L. (2003). Informal investment in Canada: Financing small business growth. *Journal of Small Business & Entrepreneurship, 16*(3–4), 13–40.

Hair, J. F., Ringle, C. M., & Sarstedt, M. (2011). PLS-SEM: Indeed a silver bullet. *Journal of Marketing Theory and Practice, 19*(2), 139–152.

Harrison, R. T., Dibben, M. R., & Mason, C. M. (1997). The role of trust in the informal investor's investment decision: An exploratory analysis. *Entrepreneurship Theory and Practice, 21*(4), 63–81.

Harrison, R. T., & Mason, C. M. (2000). Venture capital market complementarities: The links between business angels and venture capital funds in the United Kingdom. *Venture Capital: An International Journal of Entrepreneurial Finance, 2*(3), 223–242.

Hayes, A. F. (2009). Beyond Baron and Kenny: Statistical mediation analysis in the new millennium. *Communication monographs, 76*(4), 408–420.

Hulland, J. (1999). Use of partial least squares (PLS) in strategic management research: A review of four recent studies. *Strategic Management Journal, 20*(2), 195–204.

Kaiser, D. G., Lauterbach, R., & Verweyen, J. K. (2007). Venture capital financing from an entrepreneur's perspective. *The International Journal of Entrepreneurship and Innovation, 8*(3), 199–207.

Klačmer Čalopa, M., Horvat, J., & Lalić, M. (2014). Analysis of financing sources for start-up companies. *Management: Journal of Contemporary Management Issues, 19*(2), 19–44.

Kollmann, T., Kuckertz, A., & Middelberg, N. (2014). Trust and controllability in venture capital fundraising. *Journal of Business Research, 67*(11), 2411–2418.

Kotha, R., & George, G. (2012). Friends, family, or fools: Entrepreneur experience and its implications for equity distribution and resource mobilization. *Journal of Business Venturing, 27*(5), 525–543.

Lounsbury, M., & Glynn, M. A. (2001). Cultural entrepreneurship: Stories, legitimacy, and the acquisition of resources. *Strategic Management Journal, 22*(6–7), 545–564.

Lyubomirsky, S., King, L., & Diener, E. (2005). The benefits of frequent positive affect: Does happiness lead to success? *Psychological Bulletin, 131*(6), 803–855.

Maccoby, M. (2000). Narcissistic leaders: The incredible pros, the inevitable cons. *Harvard Business Review, 78*(1), 68–78.

Maccoby, M. (2003). *The productive narcissist: The promise and peril of visionary leadership.* New York, NY: Broadway Books.

MacMillan, I. C., Siegel, R., & Narasimha, P. S. (1985). Criteria used by venture capitalists to evaluate new venture proposals. *Journal of Business Venturing, 1*(1), 119–128.

Mason, C. M., & Harrison, R. T. (2003). "Auditioning for money": What do technology investors look for at the initial screening stage? *The Journal of Private Equity, 6*(2), 29–42.

Mason, C. M., & Stark, M. (2004). What do investors look for in a business plan? A comparison of the investment criteria of bankers, venture capitalists and business angels. *International Small Business Journal, 22*(3), 227–248.

Maxwell, A. L., Jeffrey, S. A., & Lévesque, M. (2011). Business angel early stage decision making. *Journal of Business Venturing, 26*(2), 212–225.

Mayhew, B. W., & Pike, J. E. (2004). Does investor selection of auditors enhance auditor independence? *The Accounting Review, 79*(3), 797–822.

Miller, D. (2015). A downside to the entrepreneurial personality? *Entrepreneurship Theory and Practice, 39*(1), 1–8.

Murnieks, C. Y., Sudek, R., & Wiltbank, R. (2015). The role of personality in angel investing. *The International Journal of Entrepreneurship and Innovation, 16*(1), 19–31.

O'Keefe, D. J. (2002). *Persuasion: Theory and research* (2nd ed.). Thousand Oaks, CA: SAGE.

Parhankangas, A., & Ehrlich, M. (2014). How entrepreneurs seduce business angels: An impression management approach. *Journal of Business Venturing, 29*(4), 543–564.

Paulhus, D. L., & Williams, K. M. (2002). The dark triad of personality: Narcissism, Machiavellianism, and psychopathy. *Journal of Research in Personality, 36*(6), 556–563.

Payne, W. H., & Macarty, M. J. (2002). The anatomy of an angel investing network: Tech Coast Angels. *Venture Capital: An International Journal of Entrepreneurial Finance, 4*(4), 331–336.

Perloff, R. M. (2008). *The dynamics of persuasion: Communication and attitudes in the 21st century.* New York, NY: Routledge.

Prasad, D., G. Vozikis, & Bruton, G. (2001). Commitment signals in the interaction between business angels and entrepreneurs. In G. Libecap (Ed.), *Entrepreneurial inputs and outcomes: New studies of entrepreneurship in the United States* (Vol. 13, pp. 45–69). Oxford, UK: Emerald Group Publishing Limited.

Sedikides, C., Rudich, E. A., Gregg, A. P., Kumashiro, M., & Rusbult, C. (2004). Are normal narcissists psychologically healthy? Self-esteem matters. *Journal of Personality and Social Psychology, 87*(3), 400–416.

Short, J. C., & Palmer, T. B. (2008). The application of DICTION to content analysis research in strategic management. *Organizational Research Methods, 11*(4), 727–752.

Sudek, R. (2006). Angel investment criteria. *Journal of Small Business Strategy, 17*(2), 89–104.

Van Kleef, G. A., De Dreu, C. K., & Manstead, A. S. (2010). An interpersonal approach to emotion in social decision making: The emotions as social information model. *Advances in Experimental Social Psychology, 42*(1), 45–96.

Van Osnabrugge, M. (2000). A comparison of business angel and venture capitalist investment procedures: An agency theory-based analysis. *Venture Capital: An International Journal of Entrepreneurial Finance, 2*(2), 91–109.

Wallmeroth, J., Wirtz, P., & Groh, A. P. (2018). Venture capital, angel financing, and crowdfunding of entrepreneurial ventures: A literature review. *Foundations and Trends® in Entrepreneurship, 14*(1), 1–129.

Zacharakis, A. L., & Meyer, G. D. (1998). A lack of insight: Do venture capitalists really understand their own decision process? *Journal of Business Venturing, 13*(1), 57–76.

Zhao, H., & Seibert, S. E. (2006). The Big Five personality dimensions and entrepreneurial status: A meta-analytical review. *Journal of Applied Psychology, 91*(2), 259–271.

Zhao, H., Seibert, S. E., & Lumpkin, G. T. (2010). The relationship of personality to entrepreneurial intentions and performance: A meta-analytic review. *Journal of Management, 36*(2), 381–404.

6. Entrepreneurial personality and the choice of seriality

6.1 INTRODUCTION

This chapter aims to investigate how narcissism affects the way entrepreneurs create value by founding more than one firm. Entrepreneurs possess the skills to identify and take advantage of multiple business opportunities (Parker, 2014). Serial entrepreneurs are characterized by a tendency to exploit these opportunities in sequence (Kuura, Blackburn, & Lundin, 2014; Westhead, Ucbasaran, & Wright, 2003). Such behavior represents the entrepreneurs' continuous desire to depart from their current business and create a new one (Wright, Westhead, Alsos, & Ucbasaran, 2007). An entrepreneurial addiction is thereby established, and they feel the urge to leave when they see that the opportunities of the existing business have been exhausted and their goals have already been achieved (DeTienne & Cardon, 2012). Entrepreneurial addiction is linked to sensations, motivations, and rewards (both extrinsic and financial) originating from the activity of creating a new business. Sensations are related to the entrepreneur's feelings of excitement, fear, and uncertainty (Spivack, McKelvie, & Haynie, 2014). On the other hand, motivation and extrinsic rewards are associated with the power, status, and social acceptance arising from the success in entrepreneurial activities (Carsrud & Brännback, 2011). Finally, financial rewards are predictors of opportunity identification. Entrepreneurs, in fact, will prefer opportunities that provide a greater financial payback (Carter, 2011; DeTienne, McKelvie, & Chandler, 2015). Serial entrepreneurship is connected to learning by doing, based on previous entrepreneurial experience (Parker, 2013). Serial entrepreneurs may be described as incubators; they are strong in venture growth, but they are not interested in maintaining/retaining such a venture.

While prior literature provides a good general understanding of the individuals' motivation pushing them to pursue their entrepreneurial ideas (Gordon, Davidsson, & Steffens, 2009; Spivack et al., 2014;

Ucbasaran, Westhead, Wright, & Flores, 2010), the psychological ante-cedents to the individual decision to become a serial entrepreneur are currently being investigated (Navis & Ozbek, 2016; Shane & Nicolaou, 2015). Only a few papers highlight the role of entrepreneurs' person-ality traits in their choice to pursue a seriality path. When referring to entrepreneurial creativity and serial entrepreneurship behaviors, Shane and Nicolaou (2015) suggest that creative personalities, due to genetic factors, possess a higher ability to identify new opportunities and start a business. By analyzing a sample comprising 5293 entrepreneurs located in Germany, Caliendo, Fossen, and Kritikos (2014) show that openness to experience, extraversion, and emotional stability increase the probabil-ity of starting another new business, while risk tolerance, locus of control, and trust have strong partial effects on entry decisions.

In the present chapter, we aim to understand whether entrepreneurial narcissism represents an antecedent to serial entrepreneurial behavior. As stated in the preceding chapters, a narcissist is commonly described as an arrogant, self-important and grandiose individual who tends to overestimate his or her abilities (Campbell, Goodie, & Foster, 2004; Gardner & Pierce, 2011; Wales, Patel, & Lumpkin, 2013). We assume that narcissism is not just a negative (i.e., destructive) trait, but also has a constructive side (Maccoby, 2003). In particular, narcissistic people are motivated and motivators, as well as being competitive, charismatic, passionate, and persevering (Maccoby, 2000, 2003). Narcissism is some-times confused with overconfidence and hubris due to some overlapping features (Engelen, Neumann, & Schmidt, 2016; Lubit, 2002). However, overconfidence is a cognitive bias whose effects only capture a small part of an individual's processes of thinking (i.e., only behavior) (Galasso & Simcoe, 2011), while narcissism embraces the full spectrum of an individual's thoughts, including emotions and behaviors, and therefore it is a personality trait (Bollaert & Petit, 2010). According to the existing literature on human personality psychology, hubris has a distinct psy-chological orientation compared to narcissism (Tang, Mack, & Chen, 2018). As opposed to narcissistic entrepreneurs, hubristic individuals do not need social attention and plaudits since they are not concerned with what others think of them due to an overconfidence in their abilities (Chatterjee & Hambrick, 2011; Petit & Bollaert, 2012).

In this chapter, we draw on dispositional theory (Davis-Blake & Pfeffer, 1989), underlining how entrepreneurs' traits affect their attitudes and behavior. Our focus is on entrepreneurs who are business owners and who have started or acquired a business (Parker, 2004). Using a cross-industry sample of 343 small business entrepreneurs, those possessing a high level of narcissism are shown to be likely to become serial entrepreneurs.

6.2   THE ROLE OF ENTREPRENEURIAL NARCISSISM IN SERIAL ENTREPRENEURSHIP

Entrepreneurs engage in serial entrepreneurial behavior because they want to "seize the moment" or due to an addiction to starting new ventures. The entrepreneur is able to recognize and estimate the value of opportunities by means of their previous experience (Gottschalk, Greene, & Müller, 2017), which provides them with the required capabilities to avoid obstacles and choose the best opportunity to pursue (Short, Ketchen Jr., Shook, & Ireland, 2010). Skills and credibility acquired from previous entrepreneurial experience further facilitate access to financial resources, also due to the entrepreneur's wider relational network with venture capitalists (Ucbasaran, Baldacchino, & Lockett, 2015). However, a new situation might require a different know-how; therefore, applying prior experiential learning may not always be straightforward (Cassar, 2014).

It is possible to divide serial entrepreneurship into two broad groups: venture repeaters and opportunist serial venture creators (Taplin, 2004). Entrepreneurs who tend to be reactive and show the ability to embark on another venture by identifying business alternatives in the same sector belong to the first category (Welsch, 2004). Entrepreneurs aiming for venture growth belong to the second category. The latter are focused on capital gains and their efforts are directed at overcoming the challenges posed by business development. Unlike the first category, they are proactive in the search for more suitable opportunities between the departure from the existing firm and the creation or acquisition of the next one (Wright, Robbie, & Ennew, 1997).

To explore the role of narcissism on entrepreneurial seriality, we propose three mechanisms regulating narcissism: (1) achievement effect; (2) optimism effect; and (3) independence effect. First, achievement effect refers to the tendency of narcissistic entrepreneurs to pursue their clear vision whatever the cost. Success and achievement are narcissists' main goals as entrepreneurs, since realization feeds their feelings of grandiosity (Maccoby, 2000). They see themselves as unique, original, and often, superior to others, and they use their business to satisfy their desires and preferences (Maccoby, 2003). Serial entrepreneurs are moved and motivated by this achievement effect to exploit innovative, original ideas and launch projects, taking risks and dealing with several challenges to pursue personal goals. Successful experience and accumulated skills lay the foundations and encourage serial entrepreneurs to embark on or acquire a new venture, making them believe in their greater chances of success in founding subsequent firms.

Optimism effect refers to the way narcissistic entrepreneurs see the future and perceive opportunities. Given their singular consideration of themselves and their capacities (Maccoby, 2000), narcissist entrepreneurs are prone to embarking on hazardous actions (Pan & Yu, 2017). When facing firm failure, however, the narcissist entrepreneur rarely blames themselves. Therefore, optimism can be a valuable means for the serial entrepreneur to develop a certain resilience to failure; it favors a more accurate perception of market opportunities, thus allowing subsequent ventures to enter the appropriate market segment.

By independence effect we refer to the tendency of narcissistic entrepreneurs to act independently. They are driven by a strong desire to break free from the rules and others' control (Chatterjee & Hambrick, 2007). This effect could enhance their propensity to seriality since it increases their psychological well-being and satisfies their urge for control and independence. In the extreme, however, there might be behavioral addiction to entrepreneurial activity.

These three advantageous effects show that high levels of entrepreneur narcissism can have a positive impact on seriality. Therefore, we hypothesize the following:

Hypothesis 1 (H_1): Entrepreneurs' narcissism is positively related to entrepreneurs' seriality.

6.3   EMPIRICAL STRATEGY

6.3.1   Sample and Procedure

The present study exploits survey data on small business entrepreneurs in Italy, France, China, USA, and Denmark. An entrepreneur can be defined as the most influential member (i.e., decision-maker) in a firm. We decided to select small businesses founded between 2008 and 2015, using different criteria depending on their home country. Italian firms were randomly sampled among those included in the Italian Chamber of Commerce register; the French firms were selected from those listed on myFrenchStartup website; finally, Chinese, US, and Danish firms were sampled consulting the angel.co website. The initial sample included 1000 firms; we collected a total of 343 answers (response rate 34.3 percent). Entrepreneurs were contacted using various channels. For those registered on LinkedIn, we used our personal LinkedIn profiles to introduce ourselves, explain our study, and send them a link to the electronic survey. In other cases, the entrepreneurs were contacted via Facebook, Viadeo, or their email address. Surveys were administered between January 2016 and April 2017; three follow-up reminder emails were sent at intervals during that period. We used Google Survey tools as the survey platform. However, for the Chinese sample, due to the restrictions on the use of Google in the Chinese territory, we employed WebSurveyCreator tools.

6.3.2   Measures

To distinguish between habitual and novice entrepreneurs, our sample was asked the following question: "Have you ever set up one or more firms before or after founding this firm?" If the answer was yes, the entrepreneurs were asked whether they currently or previously owned another firm. We attributed a value of one to affirmative answers, and a value of zero to negative ones; a dummy variable was constructed to categorize the respondent as a serial entrepreneur.

The Narcissistic Personality Inventory (NPI-16) was used to measure entrepreneur narcissism. This questionnaire was implemented by Ames, Rose, and Anderson (2006), and it includes 16 items with two statement options: one is consistent with narcissism while the other is not. The respondent's task is to indicate the level of correspondence between the statement and his or her personality (from 1 = totally disagree to 5 = fully agree). The original NPI-16 is in English, therefore a rigorous back-translation technique (Brislin, 1980) was used to ensure an accurate translation into Italian, French, and Chinese.

6.4   RESULTS

Table 6.1 presents the descriptive statistics and the Spearman's correlation of the variables in our sample.

Table 6.1   *Descriptive statistics and Spearman's correlation*

	Variable	Mean	SD	Min	Max	1	2	3	4
	Entrepreneur seriality	0.335	0.472	0	1				
	Entrepreneur narcissism								
1	Narcissism_5	2.411	1.154	1	5	1			
2	Narcissism_13	2.875	1.302	1	5	0.365***	1		
3	Narcissism_14	2.391	1.155	1	5	0.567***	0.344***	1	
4	Narcissism_16	2.755	1.233	1	5	0.344***	0.519***	0.397***	1

Note: $N = 343$; *** $p < 0.001$.

We tested our hypothesis using Smart PLS and following the recommendations of Hulland (1999), who suggests testing the adequacy of the measurement model while assessing the structural model. With regard to adequacy of the measurement model, we controlled the individual item reliability of the narcissism variable by calculating: Cronbach's alpha ($\alpha = 0.742 >$ the required value of 0.70; Nunnally & Bernstein, 1994); composite reliability (CR = 0.834 > the acceptable value of 0.70; Fornell & Larcker, 1981); and the average variance extracted (AVE = 0.557 > the required value of 0.50; Fornell & Larcker, 1981). Moreover, convergent validity was evaluated by extracting the factor and cross-loadings of all the indicator items to their respective latent constructs. Table 6.2 summarizes these results, indicating that all items load on their respective construct from a lower bound of 0.70 to an upper bound of 0.81; they load more highly on their respective construct than on any other.

Table 6.2   *Factor loadings and cross-loadings*

	Entrepreneur Narcissism	Entrepreneur Seriality
Narcissism_5	*0.708*	0.089
Narcissism_13	*0.817*	0.140
Narcissism_14	*0.731*	0.091
Narcissism_16	*0.725*	0.106
Entrepreneur seriality	0.147	*1.000*

Note: Factor loadings are shown in italic.

Finally, the bootstrapping method (Hayes, 2009) was used to assess the structural model. In the present case, 5000 bootstrap samples with replacement were requested (Hair, Ringle, & Sarstedt, 2011). Figure 6.1 depicts the structural model results. The beta path coefficient is positive and statistically significant ($\beta = 0.146$, $t = 2.849$, $p < 0.01$), supporting Hypothesis 1.

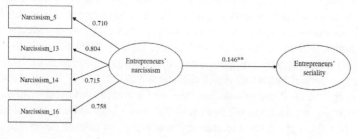

Note: **$p < 0.01$.

Figure 6.1   The relationship between entrepreneurs' narcissism and seriality

6.5   DISCUSSION AND CONCLUSION

The effect that entrepreneur narcissism has on entrepreneur seriality was investigated. Seriality in this context refers to the entrepreneurial addiction that leads an entrepreneur to depart from a firm when all the opportunities appear exhausted and the goals achieved to create a new firm with different objectives (DeTienne, 2010). Entrepreneur narcissism was shown to have a positive effect on entrepreneur seriality: high levels of narcissism correspond to a high propensity to seriality.

This chapter makes a valuable contribution to the research on entrepreneurial psychology. We provide evidence of the existence of some psychological factors that shape individual decisions and actions, responding to the call for a more in-depth explanation of the relationship between serial entrepreneurialism and personality trait differences. Our work and the achieved results highlight that entrepreneur narcissism has a strong influence on the choice to be a serial entrepreneur. We can conclude that during the new venture creation process, entrepreneurs need to consider their personal characteristics or resources (Zhao, Seibert, & Lumpkin,

2010) in order to develop critical organizational resources and capabilities (Brush, Greene, & Hart, 2001). Successful entrepreneurial endeavors require entrepreneurs to know how to use their skills (Markman & Baron, 2003); they must make decisions every day and be able to deal with failure (Politis, 2008).

The present chapter has several implications for entrepreneurial psychology, greatly contributing to the research on serial entrepreneurship. We add to the understanding of personality traits that influence entrepreneur behaviors, responding to a call for more thorough explanation of the connection between psychological traits and entrepreneurship domains (Baron & Ward, 2004; Navis & Ozbek, 2016; Spivack et al., 2014). Prior works investigate how entrepreneurs' knowledge and skills lead to certain behaviors (Gottschalk et al., 2017; Lin & Wang, 2018; Parker, 2014). Although studies on serial entrepreneurial behavior are increasing, we lack knowledge about the antecedents to these behaviors. We fill this gap in the literature by analyzing the role of entrepreneur narcissism and offering a more comprehensive understanding of entrepreneur psychology.

Our results also have practical implications. Our findings suggest that serial entrepreneurs should take their personality traits into account since they are essential for the evaluation and success of a new opportunity. This has implications for investors as well. Angel investors, venture capitalists, and banks should consider personality and prior experience as a proxy for firm founders' underlying entrepreneurial competence. Ultimately, the present work has implications for practitioners and policy-makers. In fact, to provide better targeted support for entrepreneurship they should consider entrepreneurs' personal information, based on our finding that different types of entrepreneurs perform differently.

This chapter has some limitations that suggest directions for further research. First, data do not provide information on the length of time the entrepreneur was involved in the previous new firm(s). Temporal permanence could be used to measure entrepreneurial seriality and as a proxy to check whether personality or human capital are associated with permanence. We also lack information on the composition (personality traits and human capital characteristics) of the top management team. It would be interesting to investigate the relational dynamics within this team and whether the personality and skills of certain individuals influence its strategic choices. In line with Gottschalk et al. (2017), the abilities and skills of team members could encourage mutual learning and open thinking, but, in the presence of overly strong or weak personalities, this might lead to uniformity of thinking, which could in turn endanger the firm. Sample composition represents another limitation of our study. Future work could include US and Danish entrepreneurs as well as entrepreneurs from other areas, such as Africa, to examine cultural effect on the choice to be a serial entrepreneur.

REFERENCES

Ames, D. R., Rose, P., & Anderson, C. P. (2006). The NPI-16 as a short measure of narcissism. *Journal of Research in Personality, 40*(4), 440–450.
Baron, R. A., & Ward, T. B. (2004). Expanding entrepreneurial cognition's toolbox: Potential contributions from the field of cognitive science. *Entrepreneurship Theory and Practice, 28*(6), 553–573.
Bollaert, H., & Petit, V. (2010). Beyond the dark side of executive psychology: Current research and new directions. *European Management Journal, 28*(5), 362–376.
Brislin, R. W. (1980). Translation and content analysis of oral and written material. In H. C. Triandis & J. W. Berry (Eds.), *Handbook of cross-cultural psychology: Methodology* (pp. 349–444). Boston, MA: Allyn & Bacon.
Brush, C. G., Greene, P. G., & Hart, M. M. (2001). From initial idea to unique advantage: The entrepreneurial challenge of constructing a resource base. *Academy of Management Perspectives, 15*(1), 64–78.
Caliendo, M., Fossen, F., & Kritikos, A. S. (2014). Personality characteristics and the decisions to become and stay self-employed. *Small Business Economics, 42*(4), 787–814.
Campbell, W. K., Goodie, A. S., & Foster, J. D. (2004). Narcissism, confidence, and risk attitude. *Journal of Behavioral Decision Making, 17*(4), 297–311.
Carsrud, A., & Brännback, M. (2011). Entrepreneurial motivations: What do we still need to know? *Journal of Small Business Management, 49*(1), 9–26.
Carter, S. (2011). The rewards of entrepreneurship: Exploring the incomes, wealth, and economic well-being of entrepreneurial households. *Entrepreneurship Theory and Practice, 35*(1), 39–55.
Cassar, G. (2014). Industry and startup experience on entrepreneur forecast performance in new firms. *Journal of Business Venturing, 29*(1), 137–151.
Chatterjee, A., & Hambrick, D. C. (2007). It's all about me: Narcissistic chief executive officers and their effects on company strategy and performance. *Administrative Science Quarterly, 52*(3), 351–386.
Chatterjee, A., & Hambrick, D. C. (2011). Executive personality, capability cues, and risk taking: How narcissistic CEOs react to their successes and stumbles. *Administrative Science Quarterly, 56*(2), 202–237.
Davis-Blake, A., & Pfeffer, J. (1989). Just a mirage: The search for dispositional effects in organizational research. *Academy of Management Review, 14*(3), 385–400.
DeTienne, D. R. (2010). Entrepreneurial exit as a critical component of the entrepreneurial process: Theoretical development. *Journal of Business Venturing, 25*(2), 203–215.

DeTienne, D. R., & Cardon, M. S. (2012). Impact of founder experience on exit intentions. *Small Business Economics, 38*(4), 351–374.

DeTienne, D. R., McKelvie, A., & Chandler, G. N. (2015). Making sense of entrepreneurial exit strategies: A typology and test. *Journal of Business Venturing, 30*(2), 255–272.

Engelen, A., Neumann, C., & Schmidt, S. (2016). Should entrepreneurially oriented firms have narcissistic CEOs? *Journal of Management, 42*(3), 698–721.

Fornell, C., & Larcker, D. F. (1981). Evaluating structural equation models with unobservable variables and measurement error. *Journal of Marketing Research, 18*(1), 39–50.

Galasso, A., & Simcoe, T. S. (2011). CEO overconfidence and innovation. *Management Science, 57*(8), 1469–1484.

Gardner, D. G., & Pierce, J. L. (2011). A question of false self-esteem: Organization-based self-esteem and narcissism in organizational contexts. *Journal of Managerial Psychology, 26*(8), 682–699.

Gordon, S. R., Davidsson, P., & Steffens, P. R. (2009). *Novice vs habitual entrepreneurship: Differences in motivations, actions and expectations* [Paper presentation]. AGSE International Entrepreneurship Research Exchange, University of Adelaide, Australia.

Gottschalk, S., Greene, F. J., & Müller, B. (2017). The impact of habitual entrepreneurial experience on new firm closure outcomes. *Small Business Economics, 48*(2), 303–321.

Hair, J. F., Ringle, C. M., & Sarstedt, M. (2011). PLS-SEM: Indeed a silver bullet. *Journal of Marketing Theory and Practice, 19*(2), 139–152.

Hayes, A. F. (2009). Beyond Baron and Kenny: Statistical mediation analysis in the new millennium. *Communication monographs, 76*(4), 408–420.

Hulland, J. (1999). Use of partial least squares (PLS) in strategic management research: A review of four recent studies. *Strategic Management Journal, 20*(2), 195–204.

Kuura, A., Blackburn, R. A., & Lundin, R. A. (2014). Entrepreneurship and projects – linking segregated communities. *Scandinavian Journal of Management, 30*(2), 214–230.

Lin, S., & Wang, S. (2018). How does the age of serial entrepreneurs influence their re-venture speed after a business failure? *Small Business Economics, 52*, 651–666.

Lubit, R. (2002). The long-term organizational impact of destructively narcissistic managers. *The Academy of Management Executive, 16*(1), 127–138.

Maccoby, M. (2000). Narcissistic leaders: The incredible pros, the inevitable cons. *Harvard Business Review, 78*(1), 68–78.

Maccoby, M. (2003). *The productive narcissist: The promise and peril of visionary leadership.* New York, NY: Broadway Books.

Markman, G. D., & Baron, R. A. (2003). Person–entrepreneurship fit: Why some people are more successful as entrepreneurs than others. *Human Resource Management Review, 13*(2), 281–301.

Navis, C., & Ozbek, O. V. (2016). The right people in the wrong places: The paradox of entrepreneurial entry and successful opportunity realization. *Academy of Management Review, 41*(1), 109–129.

Nunnally, J. C., & Bernstein, I. H. (1994). *Psychometric theory* (3rd ed.). New York, NY: McGraw-Hill.

Pan, Q.-Q., & Yu, F. (2017). The influential effects of narcissism leadership and its managerial implications. In L. Liu (Ed.), *Humanity and social science: Proceedings of the International Conference on Humanity and Social Science (ICHSS2016)* (pp. 48–54). Shanghai: World Scientific Publishing.

Parker, S. C. (2004). *The economics of self-employment and entrepreneurship.* Cambridge, UK: Cambridge University Press.

Parker, S. C. (2013). Do serial entrepreneurs run successively better-performing businesses? *Journal of Business Venturing, 28*(5), 652–666.

Parker, S. C. (2014). Who become serial and portfolio entrepreneurs? *Small Business Economics, 43*(4), 887–898.

Petit, V., & Bollaert, H. (2012). Flying too close to the sun? Hubris among CEOs and how to prevent it. *Journal of Business Ethics, 108*(3), 265–283.

Politis, D. (2008). Does prior start-up experience matter for entrepreneurs' learning? A comparison between novice and habitual entrepreneurs. *Journal of Small Business and Enterprise Development, 15*(3), 472–489.

Shane, S., & Nicolaou, N. (2015). Creative personality, opportunity recognition and the tendency to start businesses: A study of their genetic predispositions. *Journal of Business Venturing, 30*(3), 407–419.

Short, J. C., Ketchen Jr., D. J., Shook, C. L., & Ireland, R. D. (2010). The concept of "opportunity" in entrepreneurship research: Past accomplishments and future challenges. *Journal of Management, 36*(1), 40–65.

Spivack, A. J., McKelvie, A., & Haynie, J. M. (2014). Habitual entrepreneurs: Possible cases of entrepreneurship addiction? *Journal of Business Venturing, 29*(5), 651–667.

Tang, Y., Mack, D. Z., & Chen, G. (2018). The differential effects of CEO narcissism and hubris on corporate social responsibility. *Strategic Management Journal, 39*(5), 1370–1387.

Taplin, S. (2004). Serial entrepreneurship: An in-depth look at the phenomenon of habitual entrepreneurs. In H. P. Welsch (Ed.), *Entrepreneurship: The way ahead* (pp. 239–252). New York, NY: Routledge.

Ucbasaran, D., Baldacchino, L., & Lockett, A. (2015). Do it again! Recent developments in the study of habitual entrepreneurship and a look to the future. In T. Baker & F. Welter (Eds.), *The Routledge companion to entrepreneurship* (1st ed., pp. 131–145). New York, NY: Routledge.

Ucbasaran, D., Westhead, P., Wright, M., & Flores, M. (2010). The nature of entrepreneurial experience, business failure and comparative optimism. *Journal of Business Venturing, 25*(6), 541–555.

Wales, W. J., Patel, P. C., & Lumpkin, G. T. (2013). In pursuit of greatness: CEO narcissism, entrepreneurial orientation, and firm performance variance. *Journal of Management Studies, 50*(6), 1041–1069.

Welsch, H. P. (2004). *Entrepreneurship: The way ahead.* New York, NY: Routledge.

Westhead, P., Ucbasaran, D., & Wright, M. (2003). Differences between private firms owned by novice, serial and portfolio entrepreneurs: Implications for policy makers and practitioners. *Regional Studies, 37*(2), 187–200.

Wright, M., Robbie, K., & Ennew, C. (1997). Serial entrepreneurs. *British Journal of Management*, 8(3), 251–268.

Wright, M., Westhead, P., Alsos, G. A., & Ucbasaran, D. (2007). Habitual entrepreneurs. *Foundations and Trends® in Entrepreneurship*, 4(4), 309–450.

Zhao, H., Seibert, S. E., & Lumpkin, G. T. (2010). The relationship of personality to entrepreneurial intentions and performance: A meta-analytic review. *Journal of Management*, 36(2), 381–404.

7. The role of entrepreneurial personality: implications and conclusions

The role of entrepreneurial personality is attracting growing interest from management scholars, economists, psychologists, and sociologists concerned with the impact of both the bright and dark sides of entrepreneurial personality on firms' competitive advantage. This book has contributed to this stream of research by exploring whether – and if so, how and why – both the bright and dark sides of entrepreneur personality affect small business management and outcomes. Specifically, it identified entrepreneur personality traits and explored the mechanisms through which these traits influence small businesses outcomes with a special focus on entrepreneur narcissism. In particular, in this book we have analyzed how entrepreneurial personality traits affect small businesses' entrepreneurial orientation – innovativeness, risk-taking, and proactiveness (Miller, 1983); innovation outcomes – product/service or process innovations (Freeman, 1995); and financing – business angels. We have examined the impact personality traits have on the entrepreneur's decision to create value by founding more than one firm, that is, habitual entrepreneurship.

In this book we have paid a lot of attention to the study of entrepreneur narcissism and the way it influences the various phases of business life. It represents a comprehensive analysis directed at contributing to an animated debate. With regard to the impact narcissism has on small business outcomes, some researchers state that entrepreneur narcissism is detrimental to the firm since narcissism leads them to undertake unnecessary risks (Chatterjee & Hambrick, 2007) and not be attentive to objective performance cues (Chatterjee & Hambrick, 2011). In contrast, other scholars underline the existence of a positive side of narcissism that impacts positively on business performance (Judge, Piccolo, & Kosalka, 2009; Lubit, 2002; Rosenthal & Pittinsky, 2006; Wales, Patel, & Lumpkin, 2013), especially during a crisis (Patel & Cooper, 2014). Chatterjee and Hambrick (2007) find that narcissists tend to generate more extreme and irregular performance than non-narcissists, but in the end, narcissists do not generate systematically better or worse performance. In a subsequent study, Chatterjee and Hambrick (2011) show that narcissistic individuals exhibit a stronger positive relationship between social praise and risk-taking as compared to less narcissistic individuals; however, narcissism is unrelated to acquisition premium or risky outlays. The results obtained by Resick, Whitman, Weingarden, and Hiller (2009) do not show any significant relationships between entrepreneur narcissism and firm performance. On the other hand, Wales et al. (2013) find a positive relationship between entrepreneur narcissism and firm performance, also showing the existence of a partial mediation effect of entrepreneurial orientation. Patel and Cooper (2014) state that narcissistic entrepreneurs experience greater performance declines in the event of crisis periods, and greater performance gains in post-crisis periods. Finally, Reina, Zhang, and Peterson (2014) show that entrepreneur narcissism has implications for the firm's group dynamics and performance, explaining that narcissism can have either beneficial or detrimental effects depending on the entrepreneur's level of organizational identification.

Empirically, this book has made important contributions by using research and analysis techniques from a wide variety of disciplines including entrepreneurship, strategic management, entrepreneurial finance, and innovation studies. We tested our conjectures using both quantitative and qualitative analyses of original data the authors collected in a sample including Italian, French, Chinese, US, and Danish small-business entrepreneurs, personal interviews with entrepreneurs and employees, and secondary data from the Bureau van Dijk Aida and Orbis databases.

We therefore provide a comprehensive theoretical/analytical/empirical grounding for the effects entrepreneurial personality has on small businesses. This book's contributions are therefore unique, representing a step towards the development of a more complete understanding of the entrepreneur's role in a small firm.

This book also has important practical implications. From the perspective of leading consultancies and business advisors, there is a lack of knowledge and data on business issues concerning how entrepreneurial personality works. Practitioners such as entrepreneurs, investors, and educators are also interested in this issue. Through this book entrepreneurs will recognize and understand the importance and the role of personality traits and how these affect firm outcomes. Investors – business angels, bankers, public agencies, and other investors – can rely on this book to understand and recognize appropriate measures to assess personality traits when screening entrepreneurial projects. This will help them identify entrepreneurs with the potential to manage high-performing firms. This book offers hints for educators developing courses dedicated to existing and future entrepreneurs. It will support them in the process of recognizing and cultivating the entrepreneurial personality traits that are more likely to have a positive impact on a firm's outcomes.

REFERENCES

Chatterjee, A., & Hambrick, D. C. (2007). It's all about me: Narcissistic chief executive officers and their effects on company strategy and performance. *Administrative Science Quarterly, 52*(3), 351–386.

Chatterjee, A., & Hambrick, D. C. (2011). Executive personality, capability cues, and risk taking: How narcissistic CEOs react to their successes and stumbles. *Administrative Science Quarterly, 56*(2), 202–237.

Freeman, C. (1995). The "National System of Innovation" in historical perspective. *Cambridge Journal of Economics, 19*(1), 5–24.

Judge, T. A., Piccolo, R. F., & Kosalka, T. (2009). The bright and dark sides of leader traits: A review and theoretical extension of the leader trait paradigm. *The Leadership Quarterly, 20*(6), 855–875.

Lubit, R. (2002). The long-term organizational impact of destructively narcissistic managers. *The Academy of Management Executive, 16*(1), 127–138.

Miller, D. (1983). The correlates of entrepreneurship in three types of firms. *Management Science, 29*(7), 770–791.

Patel, P. C., & Cooper, D. (2014). The harder they fall, the faster they rise: Approach and avoidance focus in narcissistic CEOs. *Strategic Management Journal, 35*(10), 1528–1540.

Reina, C. S., Zhang, Z., & Peterson, S. J. (2014). CEO grandiose narcissism and firm performance: The role of organizational identification. *The Leadership Quarterly, 25*(5), 958–971.

Resick, C. J., Whitman, D. S., Weingarden, S. M., & Hiller, N. J. (2009). The bright-side and the dark-side of CEO personality: Examining core self-evaluations, narcissism, transformational leadership, and strategic influence. *Journal of Applied Psychology, 94*(6), 1365–1381.

Rosenthal, S. A., & Pittinsky, T. L. (2006). Narcissistic leadership. *The Leadership Quarterly, 17*(6), 617–633.

Wales, W. J., Patel, P. C., & Lumpkin, G. T. (2013). In pursuit of greatness: CEO narcissism, entrepreneurial orientation, and firm performance variance. *Journal of Management Studies, 50*(6), 1041–1069.

Index